BANKING IN CHINA

Books LLC®, Wiki Series, Memphis, USA, 2011. ISBN: 9781156683699. www.booksllc.net
Copyright: http://creativecommons.org/licenses/by-sa/3.0/deed.en

Table of Contents

Banking in China
Banking in the People's Republic of China 1
China Banking Regulatory Commission 4
China UnionPay 5
Four Northern Banks 7
GITIC 7
History of banking in China 7
Imperial Bank of China 11
Three Southern Banks 11

Banking in Hong Kong
Clearing House Automated Transfer System 11
Exchange Bank Association 12
Hong Kong Association of Banks 12

Banks of China
Afriland First Bank 13
Agricultural Bank of China 13
Bank of Beijing 14
Bank of China 14
Bank of Communications 17
Bank of Dalian 18
Bank of Jilin 18
Bank of Ningbo 18
Bank of Shanghai 19
China-based financial stocks in Hong Kong 19
China Bohai Bank 19
China CITIC Bank 20
China Construction Bank 20
China Development Bank 21
China Merchants Bank 23
Chinese financial system 23
Citibank (China) 28
County Bank 28
Exim Bank of China 28
Guangdong Development Bank 29
HSBC Bank (China) 29
Harbin Bank 30
Hua Xia Bank 30
Industrial Bank (China) 30
Industrial Bank Co. 30
Industrial and Commercial Bank of China 31
Minsheng Banking Corp 32
People's Bank of China 33
Ping An Bank 34
Postal Savings Bank of China 34
Shanghai Pudong Development Bank 34
Shengjing Bank 35
Shenzhen City Commercial Bank 35
Shenzhen Development Bank 35
Sili Bank 35
Taizhou Commercial Bank 36
Xiamen International Bank 36
Zhejiang Tailong Commercial Bank . 37

Chinese bankers
David Shou-Yeh Wong 37
Fang Chengguo 37
H.J. Shen 38
H. H. Kung 38
Jiang Jianqing 40
Jing Shuping 40
K. P. Chen 40
Li Ruogu 43
Li Zhaohuan 44
Lim Peng Siang 44
Xiang Junbo 45
Xiao Gang 45
Zhang Youyi 46
Zhuang Xiaotian 46

Introduction

Purchase of this book entitles you to a free trial membership in the publisher's book club at www.booksllc.net. (Time limited offer.) Simply enter the barcode number from the back cover onto the membership form. The book club entitles you to select from hundreds of thousands of books at no additional charge. You can also download a digital copy of this and related books to read on the go. Simply enter the title or subject onto the search form to find them.

Each chapter in this book ends with a URL to a hyperlinked online version. Type the URL exactly as it appears. If you change the URL's capitalization it won't work. Use the online version to access related pages, websites, footnotes, tables, color photos, updates. Click the version history tab to see the chapter's contributors. Click the edit link to suggest changes.

A large and diverse editor base collaboratively wrote the book, not a single author. After a long process of discussion and debate, the chapters gradually took on a neutral point of view reached through consensus. Additional editors expanded and contributed to chapters striving to achieve balance and comprehensive coverage. This reduced the regional or cultural bias found in many other books and provided access and breadth on subject matter otherwise little documented.

Banking in the People's Republic of China

China's banking system has undergone significant changes in the last two decades: banks are now functioning more like banks than before. Nevertheless, China's banking industry has remained in the government's hands even though banks have gained more autonomy. WTO has accepted China. The central bank of the People's Republic of China is the People's Bank of China.

The "big four" state-owned commercial banks are the Bank of China, the China Construction Bank, the Industrial and Commercial Bank of China and the Agricultural Bank of China.

History

Supervisory bodies

The People's Bank of China (PBOC) is China's central bank, which formulates and implements monetary policy. The PBOC maintains the banking sector's payment, clearing and settlement systems, and manages official foreign exchange and gold reserves. It oversees the State Administration of Foreign Exchange (SAFE) for setting foreign-exchange policies.

According to the 1995 Central Bank law, PBOC has full autonomy in applying the monetary instruments, including setting interest rate for commercial banks and trading in government bonds. The State Council maintains oversight of PBOC policies.

China Banking Regulatory Commission (CBRC) was officially launched on April 28, 2003, to take over the supervisory role of the PBOC. The goal of the landmark reform is to improve the efficiency of bank supervision and to help the PBOC to further focus on the macro economy and currency policy.

According to the official Announcement by CBRC posted on its website, the CBRC is responsible for "the regulation and supervision of banks, asset management companies, trust and investment companies as well as other deposit-taking financial institutions. Its mission is to maintain a safe and sound banking system in China."

Domestic key players

State-owned commercial banks – The 'Big Four'

In 1995, the Chinese Government introduced the Commercial Bank Law to commercialize the operations of the four state-owned banks, the Bank of China (BOC), the China Construction Bank (CCB), the Agricultural Bank of China (ABC), and the Industrial and Commercial Bank of China (ICBC).

The Industrial & Commercial Bank of China (ICBC) is the largest bank in China by total assets, total employees and total customers. ICBC differentiates itself from the other State Owned Commercial Banks by being second in foreign exchange business and 1st in RMB clearing business. It used to be the major supplier of funds to China's urban areas and manufacturing sector.

The Bank of China (BOC) specializes in foreign-exchange transactions and trade finance. In 2002, BOC Hong Kong (Holdings) was successfully listed on the Hong Kong Stock Exchange. The USD2.8 billion offering was oversubscribed by 7.5 times. The deal was a significant move in the reform of China's banking industry.

The China Construction Bank (CCB) specializes in medium to long-term credit for long term specialized projects, such as infrastructure projects and urban housing development.

The Agriculture Bank of China (ABC) specializes in providing financing to China's agricultural sector and offers wholesale and retail banking services to farmers, township and village enterprises (TVEs) and other rural institutions.

Policy banks

Three new "policy" banks, the Agricultural Development Bank of China (ADBC), China Development Bank (CDB), and the Export-Import Bank of China (Chexim), were established in 1994 to take over the government-directed spending functions of the four state-owned commercial banks. These banks are responsible for financing economic and trade development and state-invested projects.

ADBC provides funds for agricultural development projects in rural areas; the CDB specializes in infrastructure financing, and Chexim specializes in trade financing.

Second tier commercial banks

In addition to the big four state-owned commercial banks, there are smaller commercial banks. The largest ones in this group include the Bank of Communications, China CITIC Bank, China Everbright Bank, Hua Xia Bank, China Minsheng Bank, Guangdong Development Bank, Shenzhen Development Bank, China Merchants Bank, Shanghai Pudong Development Bank and Industrial Bank. The second tier banks are generally healthier in terms of asset quality and profitability and have much lower non-performing loan ratios than the big four.

City commercial banks

The third significant group in Chinese banking market is the city commercial banks. Many of them were founded on the basis of urban credit cooperatives. The first one was Shenzhen City Commercial Bank in 1995. In 1998, PBOC announced that all urban cooperative banks change their name to city commercial bank. And there are 69 city commercial banks set up from 1995 to 1998. In 2005 there were 112 city commercial banks in all of China. This number has increased though additional transformations to 140 in 2009. Most city commercial banks have strong ties to their local government and are majority or wholly state owned. Since 2005 some city commercial banks diversify their shareholders, inviting Chinese and international private companies to take minority shares, merging and cross-shareholding. Some of the banks have listed their shares. The city commercial banks market orientation is towards supporting the regional economy, but also towards financing local infrastructure and other government projects. Since 2008 a strong trend has emerged for city commercial banks to extend business beyond their home region. They are also often the main shareholder behind village and township banks (VTB). Some have founded so called small loans units to serve smaller business clients better. Taizhou City Commercial Bank, Bank of Beijing and Bank of Ningbo are examples for city commercial banks.

Trust and investment corporations

In the midst of the reforms of the 1980s, the government established some new investment banks that engaged in various forms of merchant and investment banking activities. However, many of the 240 or so international trust and investment corporations (ITICs) established by government agencies and provincial authorities experienced severe liquidity problems after the bankruptcy of the Guangdong International Trust and Investment Corporation (GITIC) in late 1998. The largest surviving ITIC is China International Trust and Investment Corporation (CITIC), which has a banking subsidiary known as China CITIC Bank.

Reforms in the banking industry

Years of government-directed lending has presented Chinese banks with large amounts of non-performing loans. According to the Central Bank's report, non-performing loans account for 21.4% to 26.1% of total lending of China's four big banks in 2002. In 1999, four asset management companies (AMC) were established to transfer the non-performing assets from the banks. The AMCs plan to repackage the non-performing loans into viable assets and sell them off to the investors.

PBOC has encouraged banks to diversify their portfolios by increasing their services to the private sector and individual consumers. In July 2000, a personal credit rating system was launched in Shanghai to be used to assess consumer credit risk and set ratings standards. This is an important move in developing China's consumer credit industry, and increase bank loans to individuals.

The central government has allowed several small banks to raise capital through bonds or stock issues. Followed the listing of Shenzhen Development Bank and Pudong Development Bank, China Minsheng Bank, then the only private bank in China, was listed on the Shanghai Stock Exchange (A-Share) in December 2000. More Chinese banks are expected to list in the next two years in order to raise capital.

The reform of the banking system has been accompanied by PBOC's decision to decontrol interest rates. Market-based interest rate reform is intended to establish the pricing mechanism of the deposit and lending rates based on market supply and demand. The central bank would continue to adjust and guide the interest rate development, which allows the market mechanism to play a dominant role in financial resource allocation.

The sequence of the reform is to liberalize the interest rate of foreign currency before that of domestic currency, lending before deposit, large amount and long term before small amount and short term. As a first step, the PBOC liberalized the interest rates for foreign currency loans and large deposits (US$3 million and over) in September 2000. Rate for deposits below US$3 million remain subject to PBOC control. In March 2002, the PBOC unified foreign currency interest rate policies for Chinese and foreign financial institutions in China. Small foreign exchange deposits of Chinese residents with foreign banks in China were included in the PBOC interest rate administration of small foreign exchange deposits, so that domestic and foreign financial institutions are treated fairly with regard to the interest rate policy of foreign exchange deposits.

As interest rate liberalization progressed, the PPOC liberalized, simplified or abandoned 114 categories of interest rates initially under control since 1996. At present, 34 categories of interest rates remain subject to PBOC control. The full liberalization of interest rates on other deposit accounts, including checking and saving accounts, is expected to take much longer. On the lending side, market-determined interest rates on loans will first be introduced in rural areas and then followed by rate liberalization in cities.

Credit and Debit cards

By the end of the first quarter of 2009, about 1,888,374,100 (1.89 billion) bank cards have been issued in China. Of these cards, 1,737,901,000 (1.74 billion) or 92% were debit cards, while the rest (150,473,100, or 150.5 million) were credit cards. In 2010 China had over 2.4 billion bankcards in circulation growing approximately 16% from the end of 2009.

At the end of 2008, China had approximately 1.84 million POS machines and 167,500 ATMs. About 1.18 million merchants in China accept banking cards.

At the end of 2008, there were 196 issuers in China that issue China UnionPay-branded cards. These issuers include the 'big four' banks (Industrial and Commercial Bank of China, the Bank of China, China Construction Bank, and the Agricultural Bank of China), as well as fast-growing second tier banks and city commercial banks, and even some foreign banks with local operations.

Most of China's state-owned commercial banks now issue dual-currency cards, allowing cardholders to purchase goods within China in RMB and overseas in US dollars (Visa/MasterCard/AmEx/JCB), Euros (Visa/MasterCard), Australian dollars (MasterCard), or Japanese yen (JCB). However, only Bank of China provides yen and Australian dollar-denominated credit cards.

According to a 2003 research study by VISA, the average per transaction purchase with a card was USD 253. Consumers used their credit cards mainly to purchase houses, vehicles, and home appliances, as well as to pay utility bills.

One major issue is the lack of a national credit bureau to provide credit information for banks to evaluate individual loan applicants. In 2002, the Shanghai Information Office and the People's Bank of China Shanghai branch established the first personal credit data organization involving 15 commercial banks. The Chinese Government, aiming to promote a nationwide credit system, has also set up a credit system research group. At present, large cities, such as Beijing, Guangzhou, Shenzhen, Chongqing, and Chengdu, are calling for a reliable credit data system. The PBOC is currently evaluating the feasibility of establishing a nationwide credit bureau.

Other obstacles include lack of merchant acceptance and a weak infrastructure for card processing. At present, only 2% of merchants in China are equipped to handle card transactions, although in some major cities like Shanghai the percentage is over 30%. China UnionPay was established to set up a national processing network connecting merchants and banks. China UnionPay has set up bankcard network service centers in 18 cities in addition to a national bankcard information switch center.

Products and services in the credit card system that the Chinese government wants to develop are credit card-related hardware, including POS and ATMs, credit card-related software for banks and merchants; and Credit and risk management training programs.

Foreign banks

China's entry into the WTO is expected to create opportunities for foreign banks. As a milestone move to honor its WTO commitments, China released the *Rules for Implementing the Regulations Governing Foreign Financial Institutions in the People's Republic of China* in January 2002. The rules provide detailed regulations for implementing the administration of the establishment, registration, scope of business, qualification, supervision, dissolution and liquidation of foreign financial institutions. They also stipulate that foreign bank branches conducting full aspects of foreign-currency business and full aspects of RMB business to all categories of clients are required to have operating capital of at least 600 million RMB (USD$ 72.3 million), of which at least 400 million RMB (USD$48.2 million) must be held in RMB and at least 200 million RMB (USD$24.1 million) in freely convertible currency.

Client restriction on foreign currency business was lifted immediately after China's entry into the WTO on December 11, 2001. Since then, foreign financial institutions have been permitted to provide foreign currency services to Chinese enterprises and individuals, and have been permitted to provide local currency business to all Chinese clients by the end of 2006. In 2007 five non-mainland banks were allowed to issue bank cards in China, with Bank of East Asia also allowed to issue UnionPay credit cards in the mainland (United Overseas Bank and Sumitomo Mitsui Financial Group have only issued cards in their home countries; they are not yet allowed to issue cards within the mainland). In May 2009 Woori Bank became the first Korean bank allowed to issue UnionPay debit cards on the mainland (it issues UnionPay credit cards in Korea only).

Furthermore, when China entered the WTO, geographic restrictions placed on RMB-denominated business was phased out in four major cities—Shanghai, Shenzhen, Tianjin and Dalian. Then, on December 1, 2002, foreign-funded banks were allowed to commence RMB-denominated business in Guangzhou, Zhuhai, Qingdao, Nanjing and Wuhan.

Electronic banking

In 1994, China started the "Golden Card Project," enabling cards issued by banks to be used all over the country through a network. The establishment of the China Association of Banks rapidly promoted the inter-bank card network and by the end of 2004, the inter-region-inter-bank network had reached 600 cities, including all prefecture-level cities and more than 300 economically developed county-level cities.

Source (edited): "http://en.wikipedia.org/wiki/Banking_in_the_People%27s_Republic_of_China"

China Banking Regulatory Commission

The **China Banking Regulatory Commission** (**CBRC**) is an agency of the People's Republic of China (PRC) authorised by the State Council to regulate the banking sector of the PRC except the territories of Hong Kong and Macau, both of which are special administrative regions.

Main functions

- Formulate supervisory rules and regulations governing the banking institutions;
- Authorise the establishment, changes, termination and business scope of the banking institutions;
- Conduct on-site examination and off-site surveillance of the banking institutions, and take enforcement actions against rule-breaking behaviors;
- Conduct fit-and-proper tests on the senior managerial personnel of the banking institutions;
- Compile and publish statistics and reports of the overall banking industry in accordance with relevant regulations;
- Provide proposals on the resolution of problem deposit-taking institutions in consultation with relevant regulatory authorities;
- Responsible for the administration of the supervisory boards of the major State-owned banking institutions; and Other functions delegated by the State Council;

Supervisory focuses

- Conduct consolidated supervision to assess, monitor and mitigate the overall risks of each banking institution as a legal entity;
- Stay focused on risk-based supervision and improvement of supervisory process and methods;
- Urge banks to put in place and maintain a system of internal controls:
- Enhance supervisory transparency in line with international standards and practices.

Regulatory objectives

- Protect the interests of depositors and consumers through prudential

and effective supervision;
- Maintain market confidence through prudential and effective supervision;
- Enhance public knowledge of modern finance though customer education and information disclosure;
- Combat financial crimes.

Supervisory and regulatory criteria
- Promote the financial stability and facilitate financial innovation at the same time;
- Enhance the international competitiveness of the Chinese banking sector;
- Set appropriate supervisory and regulatory boundaries and refrain from unnecessary controls;
- Encourage fair and orderly competition;
- Clearly define the accountability of both the supervisor and the supervised institutions; and
- Employ supervisory resources in an efficient and cost-effective manner.

Source (edited): "http://en.wikipedia.org/wiki/China_Banking_Regulatory _Commission"

China UnionPay

China UnionPay (simplified Chinese: 中国银联; pinyin: *Zhōngguó Yínlián*), also known as **UnionPay** (simplified Chinese: 银联; pinyin: *Yínlián*) or by its abbreviation, **CUP**, is the only domestic bank card organization in the People's Republic of China (PRC). Founded in March 2002, China UnionPay is an association for China's banking card industry, operating under the approval of the People's Bank of China (PBOC, central bank of China). It is also the only interbank network in China excluding Hong Kong and Macau, linking the ATMs of some fourteen major banks and many more smaller banks throughout mainland China. It is also an EFTPOS (*Electronic Funds Transfer at Point of Sale*) network.

History

With the approval of the People's Bank of China, China UnionPay was launched on March 26, 2002 in Shanghai by PBOC governor Dai Xianglong, with the Industrial and Commercial Bank of China, the Agricultural Bank of China, the Bank of China and the China Construction Bank serving as its first members. However, the concept of a unified Chinese bank card network dates back to 1993, with the formation of the "Golden Card Project" advocated by then-Chinese president Jiang Zemin. UnionPay is considered the descendant of the Golden Card Project, although attempts at unifying China's various credit card and interbank networks have been in place since the 1990s.

Use abroad

Now UnionPay card can be used in 104 countries and regions around the world. Some UnionPay Credit Cards are also affiliated with either American Express, MasterCard or Visa, and they can be used abroad as an American Express, Mastercard or Visa. UnionPay Debit Cards, however, can only be used in the UnionPay network and other networks that have signed contracts with UnionPay. Since 2006, China UnionPay cards can be used in over 100 countries outside China, including Australia, Canada, France, Germany, Japan, Malaysia, Singapore, South Korea, Switzerland, Thailand, New Zealand, the United Arab Emirates, and the United States. UnionPay cards are also making inroads into other countries' interbank networks, with some networks, such as BancNet in the Philippines, already accepting UnionPay cards at the ATM level and the point-of-sale of all SM Prime Holdings, Inc.'s Department Store, Supermarket, Hypermarket, Super Sale, Watson's, Sports Central, Appliance and Toy Kingdom.

- Afghanistan: UnionPay cards are accepted in 40 ATMs in Afghanistan main cities (from English Site > Globalization > ATM search)
- Australia: UnionPay cards are accepted at National Australia Bank ATMs and selected EFTPOS merchants, and Cashcard ATMs (a First Data company).
- Belgium: accepted in Belgium, at BNP Paribas Fortis's ATMs for Euro withdrawals.
- Brazil: accepted in Brazil, at Citibank's ATMs for Brazilian real withdrawals.
- Canada: accepted at all interac bank machines.
- Cambodia: accepted at Canadia Bank ATMs.
- Congo: accepted in 2 banks in Kinshasa city.
- Denmark: accepted in Denmark, in most shops and ATMs.
- Djibouti: accepted in 6 banks in the capital (from English Site > Globalization > ATM search)
- Egypt: accepted in nearly 100 ATMs in the main cities (from English Site > Globalization > ATM search)
- Fiji: accepted in Prouds Duty Free shops in Nadi International Airport.
- France: accepted in Printemps shops in Paris all credit agricole and Caisse d'Epargne ATMs.
- Germany: some Sparkassen (German credit unions) already accept UnionPay cards at ATMs for euro withdrawals. Accepted at some outlet shopping malls.
- Hong Kong: UnionPay cards are accepted at shops and ATMs in Hong Kong.
- Hungary:UnionPay cards are accepted at OTP ATMs in Hungary.
- Indonesia: accepted at Citibank, DBS, HSBC, ICBC and

- OCBC NISP ATMs throughout Indonesian (currently none on Borneo).
- Iraq: At the moment UnionPay cards can be used in 20 ATM in Iraq (in Baghdad, Erbil and other cities) at CUP and CSC banks. (from English Site > Globalization > ATM search)
- Italy: Up to now, UnionPay cards could be used on nearly half of the ATMs machines in Italy and at more than 40000 department stores, brand stores, and hotel and catering merchants (from the UnionPay English site main page news, in the article with the title "UnionPay cooperating with Italy Starhotels to improve UnionPay card" and from UnionPay English Site > Globalization > Merchant search.)
- Japan: accepted in Japan Post's and 7-11's cash machines and some shops (Matsumoto Kiyoshi is one of the few chains to accept UnionPay cards at all locations; most chains will only accept UnionPay cards at central city locations).
- South Korea: accepted in some bank's ATMs, and some shops.
- Malaysia: accepted in Hong Leong's cash machines.
- Mexico: Banamex ATMs service UnionPay customers for cash withdrawals in Mexican pesos.
- Mongolia: Golomt Bank ATMs service UnionPay customers for cash withdrawals in Mongolian tögrögs.
- New Zealand: UnionPay cards are accepted at the Bank of New Zealand's 420 ATM's nationwide and selected EFTPOS merchants.
- Russia: Citibank, Bank of Moscow, VTB and Uniastrum accept UnionPay cards at ATMs, Evrofinance Mosnarbank (Moscow) issues cards.
- Singapore: accepted in ATMs displaying Network for Electronic Transfers Singapore (NETS) logos.
- Switzerland: Credit Suisse accepts UnionPay cards at ATMs.
- Syrian Arab Republic: UnionPay cards accepted in nearly 100 ATMs in Syria big cities (from English Site > Globalization > ATM search)
- Thailand: Kasikorn Bank accepts UnionPay cards at ATMs (green in color) for Thai baht withdrawals as well as TMB Bank ATMs (blue and red in color).
- Turkey: UnionPay cards are accepted at the Garanti Bank's more than 2,700 ATMs and other bank ATMs bearing the UnionPay logo (all have Chinese interfaces). UnionPay cards are accepted at tens of thousands of merchants - mainly in major tourist cities and areas.
- United Arab Emirates: Mashreqbank accepts China Unionpay cards at all its ATMs and point-of-sale machines in its Merchant network.
- United Kingdom: On August 12, 2009, China Unionpay and LINK, the only national ATM network in UK, jointly held a ceremony to announce the acceptance of China Unionpay (CUP) Card at all ATMs in the LINK network. This cooperation marks the acceptance of CUP Card at all ATMs in UK.
- United States: Citibank accepts UnionPay cards at ATMs for United States dollar withdrawals. In May 2005 Discover Network announced an alliance with China UnionPay Network. The two companies have signed a long-term agreement that allows acceptance of Discover Network brand cards at UnionPay ATMs and point-of-sale terminals in China and acceptance of China UnionPay cards on the PULSE network in the U.S. As of November 1, 2007, China UnionPay cards may be accepted where Discover Network Cards are accepted in the United States, Canada, Mexico, Central America and the Caribbean. However, Discover does not support China UnionPay for e-commerce or card-not-present transactions.
- Vietnam: DongA Bank (the former East Asia Commercial Bank), Saigon Bank For Industry and Trade accepts UnionPay cards at ATMs for Vietnamese đồng withdrawal, and United Overseas Bank Ho Chi Minh Branch accepts UnionPay cards on its merchant network in Vietnam. On October 23, 2008, China Unionpay and VietcomBank, the biggest ATM and POS network in Vietnam, announced the acceptance of China Unionpay (CUP) Card at all ATMs and merchants in the Vietcombank network.

Members

UnionPay is the primary network of the following banks listed below:

- Agricultural Bank of China
- Bank of China (including its Hong Kong-based subsidiary Nanyang Commercial Bank)
- Bank of Communications (Credit cards co-issued with HSBC)
- Bank of Ningbo
- Bank of Shanghai
- Beijing Commercial Bank
- China Construction Bank
- China Everbright Bank
- China CITIC Bank
- China Merchants Bank
- China Minsheng Banking Corporation
- Guangdong Development Bank
- Huaxia Bank (Credit cards co-issued with Deutsche Bank)
- Industrial Bank (Credit cards co-issued with Hang Seng Bank)
- Industrial and Commercial Bank of China (ICBC)
- Postal Savings Bank of China (formerly known as the China Postal Savings and Remittance Bureau)
- Shanghai Pudong Development Bank (Credit cards co-issued with Citibank)
- Shenzhen Development Bank
- Shenzhen Ping An Bank
- Taizhou City Commercial Bank

Other UnionPay-affiliated organizations include certain municipal commercial banks as well as rural credit cooperatives. Other financial institutions in cities that are already capable of issuing cards will issue UnionPay cards in succession.

In addition, ten foreign banks have the right to issue UnionPay debit cards in China:
- Standard Chartered Bank
- Bank of East Asia
- Citibank
- HSBC
- Hang Seng Bank
- Woori Bank (as of May 2009)
- Development Bank of Singapore (as of July 2009)
- Hana Bank (as of November 2009)
- Wing Hang Bank (as of 2010)
- OCBC Bank (as of 2010)

While Mitsui Sumitomo Bank offers a UnionPay credit card in Japan, and United Overseas Bank offers a UnionPay credit card in Singapore. Bank of East Asia is unique in being allowed to independently issue UnionPay credit cards in both Hong Kong and the mainland. HSBC and its subsidiary Hang Seng Bank independently issue UnionPay credit cards in Hong Kong while they issue cards in the mainland in cooperation with local banks as noted above. Citibank uses the same arrangement (independently issuing UnionPay cards in Hong Kong while co-issuing with a partner in the mainland) and Deutsche Bank only has co-issued cards, with no independently-issued UnionPay credit cards.

Overall, there are 165 financial institutions that issue UnionPay cards.

Outside China, UnionPay has partnerships with other ATM networks. UnionPay has a partnership with JETCO in Hong Kong and Macau, both of which are not included in the UnionPay system, although this ended as of January 1, 2006. UnionPay also has affiliations with other banks' networks: this is identified with a UnionPay sticker being displayed usually on the door of the ATM room or on the ATM itself. The sticker has the UnionPay logo and the words "Welcome to use China UnionPay cards" displayed on the bottom in English and Chinese.

Source (edited): "http://en.wikipedia.org/wiki/China_UnionPay"

Four Northern Banks

Four Northern Banks (Chinese: 北四行) referred to the four most capitalized commercial banks in the north of the Yangtze River in the Republic of China in the 1920s, in contrast to the **Three Southern Banks** (南三行) of Southern China.

The four banks were the Yien Yieh Commercial Bank (鹽業銀行), the Kincheng Banking Corporation (金城銀行), the Continental Bank (大陸銀行) and the China & South Sea Bank (中南銀行).

See others
- Yien Yieh Commercial Bank
- Kincheng Banking Corporation
- Continental Bank
- China & South Sea Bank
- Three Southern Banks

Source (edited): "http://en.wikipedia.org/wiki/Four_Northern_Banks"

GITIC

Guangdong International Trust and Investment Corporation (**GITIC**) was one of People's Republic of China's largest state-owned companies. On January 16, 1999, its bankruptcy was the biggest in the history of the country to date.

Source (edited): "http://en.wikipedia.org/wiki/GITIC"

History of banking in China

The **history of banking in China** includes the business of dealing with money and credit transactions in China.

Early Chinese banks

Jiaozi, the world's first paper-printed currency, an innovation of the Song era (960-1279).

Chinese financial institutions were conducting all major banking functions, including the acceptance of deposits, the making of loans, issuing notes, money exchange, and long-distance remittance of money by the Song Dynasty (960-1279). In 1024, the first paper currency was issued by the state in Sichuan. The institutions of *piaohao* (票號) and *qianzhuang* (錢莊) more often cooperated than competed in China's financial market.

Piaohao

An early Chinese banking institution was called the *piaohao*, also known as Shanxi banks because they were owned primarily by natives of Shanxi. The first *piaohao* originated from the Xiyuecheng Dye Company of Pingyao. To deal with the transfer of large amounts of cash from one branch to another, the company introduced drafts, cashable in the company's many branches around China. Although this new method was originally designed for business transactions within the Xiyuecheng Company, it became so popular that in 1823 the owner gave up the dye business altogether and reorganised the company as a special remittance firm, Rishengchang Piaohao. In the next thirty years, eleven *piaohao* were established in Shanxi province, in the counties of Qixian, Taigu, and Pingyao. By the end of the nineteenth century, thirty-two *piaohao* with 475 branches were in business covering most of China.

All *piaohao* were organised as single proprietaries or partnerships, where the owners carried unlimited liability. They concentrated on interprovincial remittances, and later on conducting government services. From the time of the Taiping Rebellion, when transportation routes between the capital and the provinces were cut off, *piaohao* began involved with the delivery of government tax revenue. *Piaohao* grew by taking on a role in advancing funds and arranging foreign loans for provincial governments, issuing notes, and running regional treasuries.

Qianzhuang

Independent of the nationwide network of *piaohao* there were a large number of small native banks, generally called *qianzhuang*. These institutions first appeared in the Yangzi Delta region, in Shanghai, Ningbo, and Shaoxing. The first *qianzhuang* can be traced to at least the mid-eighteenth century. In 1776, several of these banks in Shanghai organised themselves into a guild under the name of *qianye gongsuo*. In contrast to *piaohao*, most *qianzhuang* were local and functioned as commercial banks by conducting local money exchange, issuing cash notes, exchanging bills and notes, and discounting for the local business community.

Qianzhuang maintained close relationships with Chinese merchants, and grew with the expansion of China's foreign trade. When Western banks first entered China, they issued "chop loans" (*caipiao*) to the *qianzhuang*, who would then lend this money to Chinese merchants who used it to purchase goods from foreign firms. It is estimated that there were around 10,000 *qianzhuang* in China in the early 1890s.

Entry of foreign banks

British and other European banks entered China around the middle of the nineteenth century to service the growing number of Western trade firms. The Chinese coined the term *yinhang* (銀行), meaning "silver institution", for the English word "bank". The first foreign bank in China was the Bombay-based British Oriental Bank (東藩匯理銀行), which opened branches in Hong Kong, Guangzhou and Shanghai in the 1840s. Other British banks followed suit and set up their branches in China one after another. The British enjoyed a virtual monopoly on modern banking for forty years. The Hong Kong and Shanghai Banking Corporation (香港上海匯丰銀行), now HSBC, established in 1865 in Hong Kong, later became the largest foreign bank in China.

In the early 1890s, Germany's Deutsch-Asiatische Bank (德華銀行), Japan's Yokohama Specie Bank (橫濱正金銀行), France's Banque de l'Indo-Chine (东方匯理銀行), and Russia's Russo-Asiatic Bank (華俄道勝銀行) opened branches in China and challenged British ascendancy in China's financial market. By the end of the nineteenth century there were nine foreign banks with forty-five branches in China's treaty ports.

Foreign banks enjoyed extraterritorial rights. They also enjoyed complete control over China's international remittance and foreign trade financing. Being unregulated by the Chinese government, they were free to issue banknotes for circulation, accept deposits from Chinese citizens, and make loans to the *qianzhuang*.

Government banks

After the launch of the Self-strengthening movement, the Qing government began initiating large industrial projects which required large amounts of capital. Though the existing domestic financial institutions provided sufficient credit and transfer facilities to support domestic trade and worked well with small-scale enterprises, they could not meet China's new financial demands. China turned to foreign banks for large scale and long term finance. Following a series of military defeats, the Qing government was forced to borrow from foreign banks and syndicates to finance its indemnity payments to foreign powers.

A number of proposals were made by a modern Chinese banking institution from the 1860s onwards. Li Hongzhang, one the leaders of the self-strengthening movement, made serious efforts to create a foreign-Chinese joint bank in 1885 and again in 1887.

The Imperial Bank of China (中国通商银行), China's first modern bank, opened for business in 1897. The bank was organised as a joint-stock firm. It adopted the internal regulations of HSBC, and its senior managers were foreign professionals. After the proclamation of the Republic of China, the bank changed its English name to the Commercial Bank of China in 1912. The name more accurately translated its Chinese name and removed any link to the Qing Dynasty.

In 1905, China's first central bank was established as the Bank of the Board of Revenue(大清户部银行). Three years later, its name was changed to the Great Qing Government Bank (大清銀行). Intended as a replacement for all existing banknotes, the Da Qing Bank's note was granted exclusive privilege to be used in all public and private fund transfers, including tax payments and debt settlements. Da Qing Bank was also given exclusive privilege to run the state treasury. The Board of Revenue that controlled most the central government's revenue transferred most of its tax remittance through the bank and its branches. The government entrusted the bank with the transfer of the Salt Surplus Tax, diplomatic expenditures, the management of foreign loans, the payment of foreign indemnities, and the deposit and transfer of the customs tax in many treaty ports.

Following the Xinhai Revolution of 1911, Daqing Bank was renamed the Bank of China. This bank continues to exist today.

Another government bank, the Bank of Communications (交通银行), was organised in 1908 by the Ministry of Posts and Communications to raise money for the redemption of the Beijing-Hankou Railway from Belgian contractors. The bank's aim was to unify funding for steamship lines, railways, as well as telegraph and postal facilities.

Private banks

Three private banks appeared in the late Qing period, all created by private entrepreneurs without state funding. The Xincheng Bank was established in Shanghai in 1906, followed by the National Commercial Bank in Hangzhou the following year, and the Ningbo Commercial and Savings Bank (四明銀行) in 1908. In that year, the Regulations of Banking Registration was issued by the Ministry of Revenue, which continued to have effect well after the fall of the Qing dynasty.

A lion's share of the profitable official remittance business was taken by the Daqing Bank from the *piaohao*. The *piaohao* all but disappeared following the Xinhai Revolution in 1911.

The same period saw the increasing power of private interests in modern Chinese banking and the concentration of banking capital. In Shanghai, the so-called "southern three banks" (南三行) were established. They were the Shanghai Commercial and Savings Bank (上海商業儲蓄銀行), the National Commercial Bank (浙江興業銀行), and the Zhejiang Industrial Bank (浙江實業銀行). Four other banks, known as the "northern four banks" (北四行) emerged later. They were the Yien Yieh Commercial Bank (鹽業銀行), the Kincheng Banking Corporation (金城銀行), the Continental Bank (大陸銀行), and the China & South Sea Bank (中南銀行). The first three were initiated by current and retired officials of the Beijing government, whilst the last was created by an overseas Chinese.

Note suspension incident

In 1916 the Republican government in Beijing ordered the suspension of paper note conversion to silver. With the backing of the Mixed Court, the Shanghai Branch of the Bank of China successfully resisted the order.

The Bank of China's bylaws were revised in 1917 to restrict government intervention.

Golden Age of Chinese banking

The decade from the Northern Expedition to the Second Sino-Japanese War in 1937 has been described as a "golden decade" for China's modernisation as well as for its banking industry. Modern Chinese banks extended their business in scope, making syndicated industrial loans and offering loans to rural areas.

The Nationalist government created the Central Bank of China in 1928, with Song Ziwen as its first president. The Bank of China was reorganised as a bank specialising in the management of foreign exchange while the Bank of Communications focused on developing industry.

The Bureau of Financial Supervision was set up under the Ministry of Finance, to supervise financial affairs.

Confronted with imminent war with Japan, the Chinese government took control of over 70 percent of the assets of modern Chinese banks through the notorious banking coup.

After 1949

The history of the Chinese banking system has been somewhat checkered. Nationalization and consolidation of the country's banks received the highest priority in the earliest years of the People's Republic, and banking was the first sector to be completely socialized. In the period of recovery after the Chinese civil war (1949-52), the People's Bank of China moved very effectively to halt raging inflation and bring the nation's finances under central control. Over the course of time, the banking organization was modified repeatedly to suit changing conditions and new policies.

The banking system was centralized early on under the Ministry of Finance, which exercised firm control over all financial services, credit, and the money supply. During the 1980s the banking system was expanded and diversified to meet the needs of the reform program, and the scale of banking activity rose sharply. New budgetary procedures required state enterprises to remit to the state only a tax on income and to seek investment funds in the form of bank loans. Between 1979 and 1985, the volume of deposits nearly tripled and the value of bank loans rose by 260 percent. By 1987 the banking system included the People's Bank of China, Agricultural Bank of China, Bank of China (which handled foreign exchange matters), China Investment Bank, China Industrial and Commercial Bank, People's Construction Bank, Communications Bank, People's Insurance Company of China, rural credit cooperatives, and urban credit cooperatives.

The People's Bank of China was the central bank and the foundation of the banking system. Although the bank overlapped in function with the Ministry of Finance and lost many of its responsibilities during the Cultural Revolution, in the 1970s it was restored to its leading position. As the central bank, the People's Bank of China had sole responsibility for issuing currency and controlling the money supply. It also served as the government treasury, the main source of credit for economic units, the clearing center for financial transactions, the holder of enterprise deposits, the national savings bank, and a ubiquitous monitor of economic activities.

Another financial institution, the Bank of China, handled all dealings in foreign exchange. It was responsible for allocating the country's foreign exchange reserves, arranging foreign loans, setting exchange rates for China's currency, issuing letters of credit, and generally carrying out all financial transactions with foreign firms and individuals. The Bank of China had offices in Beijing and other cities engaged in foreign trade and maintained overseas offices in major international financial centers, including Hong Kong, London, New York, Singapore, and Luxembourg.

The Agricultural Bank was created in the 1950s to facilitate financial operations in the rural areas. The Agricultural Bank provided financial support to agricultural units. It issued loans, handled state appropriations for agriculture, directed the operations of the rural credit cooperatives, and carried out overall supervision of rural financial affairs. The Agricultural Bank was headquartered in Beijing and had a network of branches throughout the country. It flourished in the late 1950s and mid-1960s but languished thereafter until the late 1970s, when the functions and autonomy of the Agricultural Bank were increased substantially to help promote higher agricultural production. In the 1980s it was restructured again and given greater authority in order to support the growth and diversification of agriculture under the responsibility system.

The People's Construction Bank managed state appropriations and loans for capital construction. It checked the activities of loan recipients to ensure that the funds were used for their designated construction purpose. Money was disbursed in stages as a project progressed. The reform policy shifted the main source of investment funding from the government budget to bank loans and increased the responsibility and activities of the People's Construction Bank.

Rural credit cooperatives were small, collectively owned savings and lending organizations that were the main source of small-scale financial services at the local level in the countryside. They handled deposits and short-term loans for individual farm families, villages, and cooperative organizations. Subject to the direction of the Agricultural Bank, they followed uniform state banking policies but acted as independent units for accounting purposes. In 1985 rural credit cooperatives held total deposits of ¥72.5 billion.

Urban credit cooperatives were a relatively new addition to the banking system in the mid-1980s, when they first began widespread operations. As commercial opportunities grew in the reform period, the thousands of individual and collective enterprises that sprang up in urban areas created a need for small-scale financial services that the formal banks were not prepared to meet. Bank officials therefore encouraged the expansion of urban credit cooperatives as a valuable addition to the banking system. In 1986 there were more than 1,100 urban credit cooperatives, which held a total of ¥3.7 billion in deposits and made loans worth ¥1.9 billion.

In the mid-1980s the banking system still lacked some of the services and characteristics that were considered basic in most countries. Interbank relations were very limited, and interbank borrowing and lending was virtually unknown. Checking accounts were used by very few individuals, and bank credit cards did not exist. In 1986 initial steps were taken in some of these areas. Interbank borrowing and lending networks were created among twenty-seven cities along the Yangtze River and among fourteen cities in north China. Interregional financial networks were created to link banks in eleven leading cities all over China, including Shenyang, Guangzhou, Wuhan, Chongqing, and Xi'an and also to link the branches of the Agricultural Bank. The first Chinese credit card, the Great Wall Card, was introduced in June 1986 to be used for foreign exchange transactions. Another financial innovation in 1986 was the opening of China's first stock exchanges since 1949. Small stock exchanges began operations somewhat tentatively in Shenyang, Liaoning Province, in August 1986 and in Shanghai in September 1986.

Throughout the history of the People's Republic, the banking system has exerted close control over financial transactions and the money supply. All government departments, publicly and collectively owned economic units, and social, political, military, and educational organizations were required to hold their financial balances as bank deposits. They were also instructed to keep on hand only enough cash to meet daily expenses; all major financial transactions were to be conducted through banks. Payment for goods and services exchanged by economic units was accomplished by debiting the account of the purchasing unit and crediting that of the selling unit by the appropriate amount. This practice effectively helped to minimize the need for currency.

Since 1949 China's leaders have urged the Chinese people to build up personal savings accounts to reduce the demand for consumer goods and increase the amount of capital available for investment. Small branch offices of savings banks were conveniently located throughout the urban areas. In the countryside savings were deposited with the rural credit cooperatives, which could be found in most towns and villages. In 1986 savings deposits for the entire country totaled over ¥223.7 billion.

Source (edited): "http://en.wikipedia.org/wiki/History_of_banking_in_China"

Imperial Bank of China

The **Imperial Bank of China** (Traditional Chinese: 中國通商銀行) was the first Chinese-owned bank modelled on Western banks and banking practices. It was founded in Shanghai by Mr. Sheng Xuanhuai in 1897 successfully operating until 1913 when it was renamed to the **Commercial Bank of China**. The "rebranding" was for political reasons following the overthrow of the last emperor Pu Yi by the Nationalists in 1911.

The manager, Andrew Maitland, was hired out of retirement from the Hongkong and Shanghai Banking Corporation. Ambitions for this bank were high, and it was proposed that it take over banknote issues throughout China. Although offices were opened in Canton (Guangzhou) and Beijing (then Peking) the Imperial Bank of China never received the full support of central government and it became marginalised.

The bank was closed down in 1952 after being taken over by the Central Government of the People's Republic of China.

Source (edited): "http://en.wikipedia.org/wiki/Imperial_Bank_of_China"

Three Southern Banks

Three Southern Banks (Chinese: 南三行) referred to the three most capitalized commercial banks in the south of Yangtze River in the Republic of China in the 1920s, in contrast to the Four Northern Banks (北四行) of Northern China. With their headquarters in Shanghai, the three banks cooperated to form the group.

The three banks were The National Commercial Bank (浙江興業銀行), the Chekiang Industrial Bank (浙江實業銀行) and the Shanghai Commercial and Savings Bank (上海商業儲蓄銀行).

Source (edited): "http://en.wikipedia.org/wiki/Three_Southern_Banks"

Clearing House Automated Transfer System

The **Clearing House Automated Transfer System**, or **CHATS**, is a Real Time Gross Settlement (RTGS) system for the transfer of funds in Hong Kong. It is operated by Hong Kong Interbank Clearing Limited, a private company jointly owned by the Hong Kong Monetary Authority (HKMA) and the Hong Kong Association of Banks. Transactions in three currency denominations may be settled using CHATS: Hong Kong dollar, euro, and US dollar. In 2005, the value of Hong Kong dollar CHATS transactions averaged HK$467 billion per day, which amounted to a third of Hong Kong's annual Gross Domestic Product (GDP); the total value of transactions that year was 84 times the GDP of Hong Kong.

History
Prior to the launch of CHATS as a RTGS system, interbank settlements in Hong Kong relied on a multi-tier system which settled in a daily net basis. About 170 banks settled with 10 banks. These 10 banks, in turn, settled with Hongkong Bank, which then settled with the HKMA in a one-to-one basis. Hongkong Bank acted as the clearing house under this system, settling payments across its books in a net basis on the day following the transactions. The HKMA decided that this did not meet international standards as set by G10's Committee on Payment and Settlement Systems; following a six-month feasibility study, in June 1994, it decided to develop CHATS as a RTGS system.

After two years of development, CHATS for Hong Kong dollars was launched on 9 December 1996. CHATS for US dollars and euros were launched on 21 August 2000 and 28 April 2003, respectively. In July 2007, the Regional CHATS Payment Services was also launched to link all participants in the three different CHATS versions for transactions involving currency exchange.

Features
CHATS, like other RTGS systems, settles payment transactions on a "real time" and "gross" basis—payments are not subjected to any waiting period and each transaction is settled in a one-to-one manner such that it is not bunched with other transactions. It is a single-tier system where participants settle with one central clearing house. Payments are final, irrevocable, and settled imme-

diately if there is sufficient funds in the participant's settlement account with the clearing house. Daylight overdraft is not offered in CHATS; payments that cannot be settled due to insufficient funds are queued. Banks are able to alter, cancel, and re-sequence payments in their queues.

Since no daylight overdraft is offered, in order for banks to avoid having to maintain large balances in their settlement accounts, which accrue no interest, so that payments are processed as soon as possible, interest-free intraday liquidity may be obtained by the banks through repurchase agreements (repos). Intraday repos that are not reversed at the end of the business day are carried into overnight borrowing.

Banks access CHATS by connecting to it via Member Bank Terminals which are provided by Hong Kong Interbank Clearing Limited. They may also develop their own software to access the CHATS terminal system provided that their software follow CHATS messaging format and protocol.

Hong Kong dollar CHATS

The HKMA, which is Hong Kong's central banking institution, acts as the clearing house for Hong Kong dollar (HKD) CHATS. All licensed banks in Hong Kong maintain HKD settlement accounts with the HKMA, and as of June 2000, restricted license banks "with a clear business need" may also open settlement accounts with the HKMA. The volume of transactions in HKD CHATS in 2007, in raw number of transactions, totaled at 5,499,494. The total value of all transactions conducted in the same year was about HK$217 trillion. As of 25 August 2008, there are 142 participating banks with HKD CHATS.

US dollar CHATS

Unlike HKD CHATS, the clearing house for US dollar (USD) CHATS is a commercial bank, Hongkong and Shanghai Banking Corporation (HSBC). In addition to obtaining intraday repos for payment settlement, participating banks may also obtain intraday liquidity via an overdraft facility provided by HSBC. Banks in Hong Kong are not required to participate in USD CHATS; they may choose to join as Direct Participants or Indirect Participants. Direct Participants maintain USD settlement accounts with HSBC for payment transactions in CHATS. Indirect Participants must conduct their payment transactions through Direct Participants. Additionally, a membership category called Indirect CHATS Users exists where its banks also conduct their payment transactions through Direct Participants. The volume of transactions in USD CHATS in 2007, in raw number of transactions, totaled at 2,121,058. The total value of all transactions conducted in the same year was about USD 2,127 billion. As of 25 August 2008, USD CHATS has 76 Direct Participant member banks, 18 Indirect Participant member banks, and 134 Indirect CHATS User member banks.

Euro CHATS

Euro CHATS is structured similarly to USD CHATS. Its clearing house is also a commercial bank, Standard Chartered Bank (Hong Kong). Participating banks may obtain intraday liquidity via an overdraft facility provided by Standard Chartered Bank. Like USD CHATS, banks in Hong Kong are not required to participate in Euro CHATS. Euro CHATS has two categories of membership, Direct Participants and Indirect CHATS Users; they function in the same manner as the categories in USD CHATS. The volume of transactions in Euro CHATS in 2007, in raw number of transactions, totaled at 18,169. The total value of all transactions conducted in the same year was about €280 billion. As of 25 August 2008, Euro CHATS has 30 Direct Participant member banks and 20 Indirect CHATS User member banks.

Source (edited): "http://en.wikipedia.org/wiki/Clearing_House_Automated_Transfer_System"

Exchange Bank Association

Exchange Bank Association was originally established in 1897 in Hong Kong as a bank association in dealing with the exchange business. It then became an organization that set interest rates on bank deposits to keep bank competition alive and balanced.

History

The association was crucial in the stabilizing of financial markets during the Colonial Hong Kong era from 1890s to 1930s. Their interest rates however, only affected banks. The 1960s and 70s would spawn new deposit-taking companies that set their own interest rates. This is one of the reason why the economy was split into a 3-tier system by 1981.

Source (edited): "http://en.wikipedia.org/wiki/Exchange_Bank_Association"

Hong Kong Association of Banks

The Hong Kong Association of Banks (Chinese language:香港銀行公會 or 銀公會 in short) (HKAB) is an association created based on a series of Bank Ordinances enacted since 1948. In 1981 the association was established and replaced the Exchange Bank Association. The ordinance provides a framework for the Hong Kong Government to exchange views with the banking sector for the further development of the industry.

Although banking licenses are granted by the Hong Kong Monetary Authority, no fully licensed bank can operate in the Hong Kong is thus subject to HKAB's rules. Its members are the banks, not their employees. HKAB is under the auspices of its member banks, which are represented by their designated representatives in general meetings. Each member bank must designate a senior executive to represent it vis-à-vis HKAB at meetings.

Source (edited): "http://en.wikipedia.org/wiki/Hong_Kong_Association_of_Banks"

Afriland First Bank

Afriland First Bank is a full service bank operating in Cameroon, Equatorial Guinea and São Tomé and Príncipe. The bank was founded in Yaoundé in 1987 under the name of Caisse Commune d'Epargne et d'Investissement. Afriland First Bank Cameroon operates 23 branches or agencies in Cameroon.

Subsidiaries or Affiliates in the following countries

- Equatorial Guinea - CCEI Bank GE
- São Tomé and Príncipe - First Bank São Tomé and Príncipe
- Democratic Republic of the Congo - Afriland First Bank DRC
- Zambia - Intermarket Bank - 80% Shareholding

Representative Offices in the following countries

- Paris, France - Afriland First Bank Paris
- Beijing, China, - Afriland First Bank China
- Brazzaville, Republic of the Congo - Afriland First Bank Congo Brazzaville

According to the 2004 annual report, the company has working partnerships with Omnifinance — a bank in Cote d'Ivoire recently acquired by Nigeria's Access Bank — and with the China Construction Bank.

Source (edited): "http://en.wikipedia.org/wiki/Afriland_First_Bank"

Agricultural Bank of China

Agricultural Bank of China Limited (**ABC**, simplified Chinese: 中国农业银行股份有限公司; traditional Chinese: 中國農業銀行股份有限公司; pinyin: *Zhōngguó Nóngyè Yínháng*), also known as **AgBank**, is one of the "Big Four" banks in the People's Republic of China. It was founded in 1951, and has its headquarters in Beijing. It has branches throughout mainland China, China Hong Kong, London, Tokyo, New York, Frankfurt, Sydney, Seoul & Singapore.

ABC has 320 million retail customers, 2.7 million corporate clients, and nearly 24,000 branches. It is China's third largest lender by assets. ABC went public in mid-2010, fetching the world's biggest ever initial public offering (IPO). In 2011, it ranks No.8th among the Top 1000 World Banks, meanwhile Forbes Global 2000 named it the 25th-largest public company in the world.

History

After the establishment of the People's Republic of China in 1949, ABC has been formed and abolished several times. In 1951, two banks of the Republic of China, Farmers Bank of China and Cooperation Bank, merged to form Agricultural Cooperation Bank, which ABC regards as its ancestor. However, the bank was merged into People's Bank of China, the central bank in 1952. The first bank bearing the name Agricultural Bank of China was founded in 1955, but it was merged into the central bank in 1957. In 1963 the Chinese government formed another agricultural bank, and it was also merged into the central bank two years later. Today's Agricultural Bank of China was founded in February 1979. It was restructured to form a holding company called Agricultural Bank of China Limited. It was listed on the Shanghai and Hong Kong stock exchanges in July 2010.

In April 2007 ABC was the victim of the largest bank robbery in Chinese history. This occurred when two vault managers at the Handan branch of the bank in Hebei province embezzled almost 51 million yuan (US$7.5 million).

2010 initial public offering

ABC was the last of the "big four" banks in China to go public. In 2010, A shares and H shares of Agricultural Bank of China were listed on the Shanghai Stock Exchange and the Hong Kong Stock Exchange respectively. Each share was set to cost between 2.7RMB and 3.3RMB per share. H shares were set to cost between HK$2.88 and HK$3.48 per share. The final share price for the IPO launch was issued on July 7, 2010. On completion in August 2010 it became the world's biggest initial public offering (IPO) surpassing the one set by Industrial and Commercial Bank of China in 2006 of US$21.9 billion.

ABC raised US$19.21 billion in an IPO in Hong Kong and Shanghai on July 6, 2010, before overallotment options were exercised. On August 13, 2010, ABC officially completed the world's largest initial public offering, raising a total of $22.1 billion after both Shanghai and Hong Kong's over-allotments were fully exercised. The IPO was once thought to be able to raise US$30 billion, but weaker market sentiment dampened the value.

CICC, Goldman Sachs, and Morgan Stanley led the Hong Kong offering, with JPMorgan, Macquarie, Deutsche Bank and ABC's own securities unit al-

so involved. CICC, Citic Securities, Galaxy and Guotai Junan Securities handled the Shanghai portion. ABC sold about 40% of the Shanghai offering to 27 strategic investors including China Life Insurance and China State Construction. They are subject to lock-up periods of 12–18 months. Eleven cornerstone investors were selected for its Hong Kong share offering, including Qatar Investment Authority and Kuwait Investment Authority, taking a combined $5.45 billion worth of shares.
Source (edited): "http://en.wikipedia.org/wiki/Agricultural_Bank_of_China"

Bank of Beijing

The **Bank of Beijing** (simplified Chinese: 北京银行; traditional Chinese: 北京銀行; pinyin: *Běijīng Yínháng*) (SSE: 601169) is a bank based in Beijing, People's Republic of China. Founded on January 8, 1996 as **Beijing City Commercial Bank** (sometimes referred to as **Beijing Commercial Bank**), it adopted its present name in January 2005. The largest shareholders of the bank include: Government of the City of Beijing, and ING from the Netherlands.
Source (edited): "http://en.wikipedia.org/wiki/Bank_of_Beijing"

Bank of China

Bank of China Limited (**BOC**) SSE: 601988 SEHK: 3988 (simplified Chinese: 中国银行; traditional Chinese: 中國銀行; pinyin: *Zhōngguó Yínháng*; often abbreviated as 中銀 or 中行) is one of the big four state-owned commercial banks of the People's Republic of China. It was founded in 1912 by the Government of the Republic of China, to replace the Government Bank of Imperial China. It is the oldest bank in China. From its establishment until 1942, it issued banknotes on behalf of the Government of the Republic of China along with the "Big Four" banks of the period: the Central Bank of China, Farmers Bank of China and Bank of Communications. Although it initially functioned as the Chinese central bank, in 1928 the Central Bank of China replaced it in that role. Subsequently, BOC became a purely commercial bank.

In December 2010, the Bank of China New York branch began offering RMB products for Americans. This is the first major Chinese bank to offer such a product currently.

History

Daqing Bank's Dalian Branch. (1910)

Bank of China Headquarters, Beijing, China. (2002) Architect: I.M. Pei

Bank of China's history goes back to 1905, when the Qing government established Daqing Hubu Bank (in Chinese: 大清户部銀行) in Beijing, which was in 1908 renamed to Daqing Bank (in Chinese: 大清銀行). When the Republic of China was established in 1912, it was further renamed as Bank of China by President Sun Yat-sen's government, adding a new role of the central bank.

After the Chinese Civil War ended in 1949, the Bank of China effectively split into two operations. Part of the bank relocated to Taiwan with the Kuomintang (KMT) government. It was privatised in 1971 to become the **International Commercial Bank of China** (中國國際商業銀行). It has subsequently merged with the **Taiwan Bank of Communications** (**Chiao Tung Bank**, 交通銀行) to become the Mega International Commercial Bank (兆豐國際商業銀行). The Mainland operation is the current entity known as the Bank of China.

It is the second largest lender in China overall, and the 5th largest bank in the world by market capitalization value. Once 100% owned by the central government, via Central Huijin Investment and National Council for Social Security Fund (SSF), an IPO of its shares took place in June 2006, the free float is at present over 26%. In the Forbes Global 2000 it ranked as the 21st-largest company in the world.

It is the most international of China's banks, with branches on every inhabited continent. Outside of mainland China, BOC also operates in 27 countries including:

- Australia, Canada, United Kingdom, Ireland, France, Germany, Italy, Luxembourg, Russia, Hungary, United States, Panama, Brazil, Japan, Republic of Korea, Singapore, Taiwan, Philippines, Vietnam, Malaysia, Thailand, Indonesia, Kazakhstan, Bahrain, Zambia, South

Africa and a branch office in the Cayman Islands.

Although it is present in the above countries/territories, its operations outside China accounted for less than 4% of the activity of the bank by both profits and assets. Mainland China accounts for 60% of the bank by profits and 76% by assets as at December 2005.

Timeline of overseas expansion

Tokyo branch.

New York branch.

Bank of China building in Singapore.

- 1917 BOC opened a branch in Hong Kong.
- 1929 BOC opened its first overseas branch in London. The branch managed the government's foreign debt, became a center for the bank's management of its foreign exchange, and acted as an intermediary for China's international trade.
- 1931 BOC opened a branch in Osaka.
- 1936 BOC opened a branch in Singapore to handle remittances to China of overseas Chinese. It also opened an agency in New York.
- 1937 At the outbreak of hostilities with Japan, Japanese forces blockaded China's major ports. BOC opened a number of branches overseas to facilitate the gathering of remittances and the flow of military supplies. BOC opened branches in Batavia, Penang, Kuala Lumpur, Haiphong, Hanoi, Rangoon, Bombay, and Calcutta. It also opened sub-agencies in Surabaya, Medan, Dabo, Xiaobo, Batu Pahat, Baichilu, Mandalay, Lashio, Ipoh, and Seremban.
- 1941 and 1942 The Japanese conquest of South East Asia forced BOC to close all overseas its branches, agencies, sub-branches and sub-agencies, except London, New York, Calcutta, and Bombay.
- 1942 BOC set up six new overseas branches, including those at Sydney, (Australia), Liverpool, and Havana, and possibly Karachi.
- 1946 BOC reopened its branches and agencies in Hong Kong, Singapore, Haiphong, Rangoon, Kuala Lumpur, Penang, and Jakarta. It moved the Hanoi agency to Saigon. At the suggestion of the Allied Forces Headquarters, it liquidated the branch in Osaka and opened a sub-branch in Tokyo.
- 1947 BOC opened agencies in Bangkok, Chittagong, and Tokyo.
- 1950 Some of the branches of Bank of China joined the bank headquartered in Beijing — i.e., Hong Kong, Singapore, London, Penang, Kuala Lumpur, Jakarta, Calcutta, Bombay, Chittagong, Karachi, and Jakarta — while others — New York, Tokyo, Havana, Bangkok, and one other, possibly Panama — opted to remain with the Bank of China headquartered in Taipei. In 1971, this bank took the name International Commercial Bank of China.
- 1963 The Burmese government nationalized all banks, foreign and domestic, including the Bank of China's Rangoon branch.
- 1971 The Bank of China transferred its two branches in Karachi and Chittagong to the National Bank of Pakistan.
- 1975 The People's Republic of Vietnam nationalized the Bank of China's branch in Saigon and the Khmer Rouge government nationalized its Phnom Phen branch.
- 1981 BOC opened a branch in New York.
- 2001 Kwangtung Provincial Bank was closed and merged under Bank of China, Singapore Branch.
- 2002 Bank of China Futures Pte Ltd wound up operations in Singapore.
- 2008 Bank of China buys 20 percent stake in La Compagnie Financiere Edmond de Rothschild (LCFR) for 236.3 million euros (US$340 million)
- 2001-2007 Massive staff layoffs and paycuts in BOC S'pore Branch.
- 2007 BOC S'pore Branch - Mr Zhu Hua asked to leave S'pore by the Monetary Authority of S'pore and rumoured to be posted to Bangkok, Thailand. For poor performance, he was replaced by Mdm Liu Yan Fen.
- 2008 Head of Settlements, Mr Chin Chuh Meng, Bank of China, was investigated involvement for Multi-Level Marketing Activities in S'pore; a scheme with some Bank of China and ex Kwangtung Bank Staff.
- 2009 Opened branches in São Paulo and Maputo. Reopened branch in Penang in October.
- 2009 People's Park Remittance Centre opened in Singapore, operating 7 days a week, offering remittance and cash exchange services.
- 2009 Ceased Sunday Banking Business in Chinatown Sub-branch in Singapore.

2005

In the runup to the IPO, BOC solicited long term investors to take strategic stakes in the company. In October 2005, the Royal Bank of Scotland Group PLC announced a $3.1 billion investment which would give the British bank control of just under 10 percent stake in the Bank of China. Further investments were made by Swiss bank UBS AG, and by Temasek Holdings Pte. Ltd, who also promised to subscribe for an additional $500 million worth of shares during Bank of China's initial public offering.

The Bank has been investigated by the United States in its money laundering probe related to the superdollars affair.

2006

- Its listing, on the Hong Kong Stock Exchange on June 1, 2006 was the largest IPO in the world since 2000, and the fourth largest IPO in the world ever, raising some US$9.7 billion in the H-share Global Offering. The Over-Allotment Option was then exercised on June 7, 2006, raising the total value of their IPO to US$11.2 billion.
- It successfully made the largest IPO in mainland China on July 5, 2006, by offering up to 10 billion A-shares on the Shanghai A Stock Exchange, or up to RMB20 billion. These were priced at RMB3.00 per share.
- BOC has bought Singapore Airlines's stake in Singapore Aircraft Leasing Enterprise, in 2007 it was renamed BOC Aviation.
- The bank held another IPO on the Shanghai Stock Exchange in 2006, raising around 20 billion yuan (US$2.5 billion).

Hong Kong

Bank of China Tower in Hong Kong.

BOC started operations in Hong Kong in 1917 and has become a major player there. It became note-issuing bank Hong Kong in 1994; in Macao, it received note-issuing status in 1995.

In 2001, BOC regrouped its Hong Kong operations into Bank of China (Hong Kong); then BOCHK listed on the Hong Kong Stock Exchange in October 2002. Two-thirds of its share capital are in free float. The bank's headquarters in Hong Kong are located in the Bank of China Tower, designed by the renowned architect I.M. Pei, and was opened to the public in 1990 as the tallest building of Hong Kong at that time.

It listed on the Hong Kong Stock Exchange (independently from BOCHK) (SEHK:3988) by floating the largest IPO in the world by any institution since 2000 on June 1, 2006, raising US$9.7 billion. The IPO attracted HK$286 billion (USD 36.7 billion) in retail orders and was the most heavily oversubscribed in the history of the Hong Kong Stock Exchange. The offer was around 76 times oversubscribed. Although some financial analysts advised caution due to the worrying amounts of non-performing loans, this hardly deterred investors. The IPO share price started at HK$2.95 per share and jumped 15% (to HK$3.40) after the first day of trading.

In 2008 the Bank of China was crowned Deal of the Year - Debt Market Deal of the Year at the *2008 ALB Hong Kong Law Awards*.

Basic facts

Bank of China branch in Dalian.

- It has over RMB 6,951.68 Billions in assets, making it part of the Fortune Global 500 for the past 17 years.
- It is the no.2 lender in China overall, the no.1 lender to non-institutions, and the no.1 foreign exchange lender. (The no.1 lender in China is the Industrial and Commercial Bank of China)
- In 2002, it made RMB52.7 billion profit, an increase of over 20 per cent from the previous year.
- Bank of China owns the 7th tallest building in the world
- All overseas branches are only affiliated with Bank of China branches in China. That means that if you deposit money to China branch, you cannot access your money in overseas branches.
- Bank of China, New York internet banking is available for US dollar accounts and online access to stop payments, wire transfers and remittances. Great Wall debit MasterCard is available to account holders.
- Bank of China, New York also operates as a functional 24/7 clearinghouse for wire transfers and stop payments (allowing real time payments to China).
- Bank of China, New York has two locations: 410 Madison (open Monday - Friday); 42 East Broadway (open seven days)

Banknotes

Although it is not a central bank, the Bank of China is licensed to issue banknotes in two of China's Special Administrative Regions. Until 1942, the Bank of China issued banknotes in mainland China on behalf of the Government of the Republic of China. Today, the Bank issues banknotes in Hong Kong and banknotes in Macau (under the Portuguese name *"Banco Da China"*), along with other commercial banks in those regions.

Ownership

As of June 7, 2006, following the Hong Kong IPO, the ownership of the Bank of China (SEHK:3988) was:
- State Administration of Foreign Exchange (an investment arm of the government of the People's Republic of China): 69.265%
- RBS China: 8.467% (4.26% for the benefit of RBS, the remainer held as custodian for the interests of billionaire Li Ka-shing)
- AFH Pte. Ltd. (a wholly owned subsidiary of Temasek): 4.765%
- National Council for Social Security Fund (PRC state pension fund): 4.576%
- UBS AG: 1.366%
- ADB: 0.205%
- Investors who received H shares from the Global Offering (IPO): 11.356%

Li Ka-shing, RBS, Temasek and UBS were contracted to hold their shares until 31 December 2008. All four sold their holdings on the open market in early January 2009.

Source (edited): "http://en.wikipedia.org/wiki/Bank_of_China"

Bank of Communications

Bank of Communications Limited (**BoCom** or **BoComm**) SEHK: 3328 SSE: 601328 (simplified Chinese: 交通银行; traditional Chinese: 交通銀行; pinyin: *Jiāotōng Yínháng*; often abbreviated as 交行), founded in 1908, is one of the largest banks in China.

History

Before 1949

The Bank of Communications was founded in 1908 (the 34th year of the Guangxu reign period, Qing Dynasty) and emerged as one of the first few major national and note-issuing banks in the early days of the Republic of China. It was chartered as "the Bank for developing the country's industries". In order to expand business into the overseas arena, the Bank opened its first Hong Kong Branch on 27 November 1934.

After 1949

Republic of China

After the Chinese Civil War ended in 1949, the Bank of Communications, like the Bank of China, was effectively split into two operations, part of it relocating to Taiwan with the Kuomintang government. In Taiwan, the bank is also known as **Bank of Transportation** (交通銀行, **Chiao Tung Bank**). It eventually merged with the International Commercial Bank of China (中國國際商業銀行), the renamed Bank of China in Taiwan after its 1971 privatization to become the Mega International Commercial Bank (兆豐國際商業銀行).

People's Republic of China

The mainland operation is the current Bank of Communications.

Following the State Council's decision to restructure the Bank in 1986, the Bank was then restructured and recommenced operations on 1 April 1987. Since then, its Head Office has been relocated from Beijing to Shanghai.

Today

Today, the Bank of Communications is amongst the top 5 leading commercial banks in China and has an extensive network of over 2,800 branches covering over 80 major cities. Apart from Hong Kong, the Bank has also established overseas branches in New York, Tokyo, Singapore and representative offices in London and Frankfurt. As of end-2002, the Bank had over 45,000 employees and a total asset reaching RMB 766.874 billion.

The Bank was awarded "The Best Bank in China" by international acclaimed magazines *Euromoney* and *Global Finance* in 1998 and 1999 respectively. According to the latest ranking of 1000 banks worldwide conducted by the authoritative magazine *The Banker*, Bank of Communications was ranked 94th, its first time to join the Top-100 list. In addition, the Feb 2003 edition of *The Banker* also ranked Bank of Communications 92nd amongst the 100 most efficient lending banks of the world.

A sub-branch of the Bank of Communications Hong Kong Branch.

Events in 2005

As of January 2005, 19.9% of the bank is owned by HSBC. An HSBC spokeswoman said HSBC Holdings Plc and its 19.9% held Bank of Communications (BoComms) affiliate, would seek to acquire a brokerage to expand their operations in China. The plan was part of HSBC's broader China expansion strategy, but "there is nothing further to disclose at the present." HSBC's operations in China include its own banking operations, its stake in BoCom and an 8% stake in Bank of Shanghai. HSBC also holds a 19.9% stake in Ping An Insurance (Group) Co of China through its wholly owned subsidiary HSBC In-

surance Holdings. The South China Morning Post today cited Peter Wong Tung-shun, executive director at The Hongkong and Shanghai Banking Corporation, as saying that the acquisition is being considered in the light of the Chinese government's reforms of the country's securities brokerages. This includes a provision allowing foreign companies to get management control of brokerage firms. Wong did not provide a timetable for any acquisition or identify any acquisition target. The Hongkong and Shanghai Banking Corp is a wholly owned HSBC subsidiary.
Source (edited): "http://en.wikipedia.org/wiki/Bank_of_Communications"

Bank of Dalian

Dalian Bank's headquarters in Qingniwaqiao, Dalian

Dalian Bank (in Chinese: 大连银行) is a commercial bank, with its headquarters in Dalian, Liaoning Province, China. It was established in 1998 as Dalian City Commercial Bank, opened its branches in Dalian City only, but changed its name to Dalian Bank in 2007 and has since opened branches in Tianjin and Beijing.
Source (edited): "http://en.wikipedia.org/wiki/Bank_of_Dalian"

Bank of Jilin

Bank of Jilin (in Chinese: 吉林银行) is a commercial bank, with its headquarters in Changchun, Jilin Province, China. It is the former **Changchun City Commercial Bank**, established in 1997, which changed its name in 2007 to Bank of Jilin, as it absorbed Jilin and Liaoyuan City Commercial Banks. It further absorbed in 2008 Tonghua, Siping, Baishan and Songyuan Commercial Banks, and opened a new branch in Yanbian.

In 2008, it also opened branches outside of Jilin Province, in Tianjin, Shanghai and Beijing.
Source (edited): "http://en.wikipedia.org/wiki/Bank_of_Jilin"

Bank of Ningbo

Bank of Ningbo Company Limited (SZSE: **002142**) is a city commercial bank in Ningbo, Zhejiang, China. As of June 2008, it operated 78 branches in Ningbo and Shanghai. Since January 2008, Bank of Ningbo has become one of the constitute stocks in Shenzhen Stock Exchange Component Index. In August 2008, the bank relocated several major departments from Ningbo to Shanghai.

It was founded in 1997 as the **Ningbo Commercial Bank**. In 2007, it changed its name to **Bank of Ningbo** and listed its shares on the Shenzhen Stock Exchange. In 2006, Singapore's Oversea-Chinese Banking Corporation took a 12.2% stake in Bank of Ningbo.
Source (edited): "http://en.wikipedia.org/wiki/Bank_of_Ningbo"

Bank of Shanghai

The Bank of Shanghai building in the Jiading district of Shanghai

Bank of Shanghai (simplified Chinese: 上海银行; traditional Chinese: 上海銀行; pinyin: *Shànghǎi Yínháng*) is a bank based in Shanghai in the People's Republic of China.

In September 1999 and December 2001, Bank of Shanghai received equity investments from International Finance Corporation, HSBC and Shanghai Commercial Bank in Hong Kong.

Source (edited): "http://en.wikipedia.org/wiki/Bank_of_Shanghai"

China-based financial stocks in Hong Kong

China-based financial stocks in Hong Kong (Traditional Chinese:中資金融股 or 六行三保, Simplied Chinese: 中资金融股 or 六行三保) is the 6 banking and 3 insurance China-based company stocks listed in Hong Kong Stock Exchange.

The 6 banks are:
- Industrial and Commercial Bank of China (SEHK: 1398, SSE: 601398)
- Bank of China (SEHK: 3988, SSE: 601988)
- China Construction Bank (SEHK: 939, SSE: 601939)
- Bank of Communications (SEHK: 3328, SSE: 601328)
- China Merchants Bank (SEHK: 3968, SSE: 600036)
- China CITIC Bank (SEHK: 998, SSE: 601998)

The 3 insurance companies are:
- China Life Insurance (SEHK: 2628, SSE: 601628)
- Ping An Insurance (SEHK: 2318, SSE: 601318)
- People's Insurance Company of China (SEHK: 2328)

Source (edited): "http://en.wikipedia.org/wiki/China-based_financial_stocks_in_Hong_Kong"

China Bohai Bank

Bohai Bank (simplified Chinese: 渤海银行; traditional Chinese: 渤海銀行; pinyin: *Bóhǎi Yínháng*) is a commercial bank in Tianjin, China. The capital of the bank is 5 billion yuan (US$616.5 million).

The bank was the brainchild of the Tianjin mayor (and previous Head of the Peoples Bank of China) Mr Dai Xiang Long who turned a national banking licence for Tianjin, that had been promised to the city in the mid 1990s, into reality and in the process kicking off an important upgrading of the Tianjin financial system. This was the 1st national banking licence to have been approved by the State Council since Minsheng Bank in 1995.

The precondition for the national licence, stipulated by the regulators, was that foreign expertise should be brought in to ensure that the bank could herald a new era for Chinese banking following the modern organisational design of western banks, in particular the risk management system and product development approach.

In turn a small set up team was formed from local bank officials, led by Mr Sun Li Guo, and a beauty contest was held for the foreign banking partner. Standard Chartered Bank was selected as Strategic investor and a 19.99% shareholding was agreed. Other investors included TEDA, Cosco, BaoSteel, SDIC, with TEDA taking the lead role with a 25% shareholding.

The first appointed official of the bank was from Standard Chartered, an Englishman, Mr Simon Page, the Chief Risk Officer who took up the post in October 2004. The Head of Wholesale Bank was a Swiss national, Mr Rolf Berweger. A group of officials and technical experts from Standard Chartered Bank joined the set up team and the preparation for the bank began under the guidance of the project director Mr Clive Haswell, pulling together business strategy, technical & IT infrastructure, policies and procedures.

In August 2005 the Chairman and Chief Executive were selected, Mr Yang Zi Lin and Mr Ma Teng and the business licence was approved on 31 December 2005. The Chief Financial Officer, Mrs Guo Rong Li, Chief Technology Officer, Mr Liu Zheng Quan, Head of Consumer Bank, Mr Phang Yew Kiat were also appointed.

The first branch opened in Tianjin on 16 February 2006 and offered basic retail banking deposit services and corporate banking lending, trade and deposit services.

Source (edited): "http://en.wikipedia.org/wiki/China_Bohai_Bank"

China CITIC Bank

China CITIC Bank (simplified Chinese: 中信银行; traditional Chinese: 中信銀行; pinyin: *Zhōng Xìn Yínháng*)(SEHK: 0998 SSE: 601998) is China's seventh-largest lender in terms of total assets. It is formerly known as **CITIC Industrial Bank**. China CITIC Bank, established in February 1987, is a nationally comprehensive and internationally oriented commercial bank. By end of October 2005, its network comprises 418 branches countrywide, and includes established correspondent relationships with 990 banks and their branches in 70 countries around the world.

China CITIC Bank is a wholly owned subsidiary of China International Trust and Investment Corporation (CITIC), with assets of RMB 576 billion (USD 71 billion). As of 2006, China CITIC Bank had a non-performing loan (NPL) ratio of 2.5% (RMB 11.1 billion). The bank's capital adequacy ratio is 9.1%.

Since the bank has been listed in the Hong Kong Stock Exchange, it performs the poorest among the all pro-PRC financial stocks. It dropped below the IPO price, HK$5.80, and closed at HK$5.79 on 5 June 2007. It is the second Hong Kong China-based financial stock which drops below the IPO price, after People's Insurance Company of China.

Source (edited): "http://en.wikipedia.org/wiki/China_CITIC_Bank"

China Construction Bank

Headquarters, China Construction Bank, Beijing

China Construction Bank (CCB) SSE: 601939 SEHK: 0939 (simplified Chinese: 中国建设银行; traditional Chinese: 中國建設銀行; pinyin: *Zhōngguó Jiànshè Yínháng*; often abbreviated as 建行) is one of the 'big four' banks in the People's Republic of China. To date, it is ranked as the nation's second largest and the eighth largest bank in the world by market capitalization and 17th largest company in the world. The bank has approximately 13,629 domestic branches. In addition, it maintains overseas branches in Frankfurt, Hong Kong, Johannesburg, New York, Seoul, Singapore, Tokyo, and Sydney, and a wholly owned subsidiary in London. Its total assets reached 8.7 trillion RMB in 2009.

History

CCB was founded on 1 October 1954 under the name of "People's Construction Bank of China" (Chinese: 中国人民建设银行; pinyin: *Zhōngguó Rénmín Jiànshè Yínháng*), and later changed to "China Construction Bank" on 26 March 1996.

In January 2002, CCB Chairman Wang Xuebing resigned from the bank after being charged with accepting bribes while he was employed with Bank of China. He was later sentenced to 12 years in prison for the crimes. In March 2005, his successor, Zhang Enzhao, resigned for "personal reasons." Just prior to his resignation, he had been charged in a lawsuit with accepting a $1 million bribe. He was later sentenced to 15 years in jail in connection with the case.

China Construction Bank Corporation was formed as a joint-stock commercial bank in September 2004 as a result of a separation procedure undertaken by its predecessor, China Construction Bank, under the PRC Company Law. Following the China Banking Regulatory Committee's approval on 14 September 2004, the next day the bank (Jianyin) became a separate legal entity, owned by the Chinese government holding company, Central Huijin Investment Company or simply Huijin.

Investment by Bank of America

In 2005, Bank of America acquired a 9% stake in China Construction Bank for $3 billion. It represented the company's largest foray into China's growing banking sector. Bank of America currently has offices in Hong Kong, Shanghai, and Guangzhou and sought to expand its Chinese business as a result of this deal.

On or about 5 June 2008, Bank of America purchased 6 billion H-shares for approximately HK$2.42 per share using call options under a formula in the initial acquisition agreement. Bank of America now holds about 25.1 billion H-shares, representing about 10.75% of CCB's issued shares. Bank of America may not sell the 6 billion shares that it purchased from Huijin using the call option before 29 August 2011 without prior consent of CCB. Bank of America still has the option to purchase additional shares.

In May 2009, speculation was raised that $7.3bn worth of CCB shares had been sold by BoA, to help bolster capital during stress testing.

International expansion

In 2006, CCB acquired Bank of America (Asia), which started in 1912 in Hong Kong as Bank of Canton, and had a subsidiary in Macao.

CCB opened a London office on 2 June 2009.

In 2008, CCB submitted an application to the NY State Banking Department and the Federal Reserve Board to establish a branch in New York City. CCB officially opened its New York branch on 6 June 2009.

China Construction Bank is a member of the Global ATM Alliance, a joint venture of several major international banks that allows customers of the banks to use their ATM card or check card at another bank within the Global ATM Alliance with no transaction fees when traveling internationally. However, handling costs and VISA processing fees may be applied. Other participating banks are:
- Barclays (United Kingdom),
- Bank of America (United States),
- BNP Paribas (France),
- Deutsche Bank (Germany),
- Santander Serfin (Spain and Mexico),
- Scotiabank (Canada) and
- Westpac (Australia and New Zealand).

Health fund

China Construction Bank investment division launched a 5 billion yuan ($731.3 million) fund called **China Healthcare Investment Fund** to focus on investments in China's rapidly growing heathcare sector. The fund focuses on investments in healthcare related sectors including pharmacy, medical equipment manufacturing, medical institutions and services. It is the first domestic investment fund specializing in investments in China's heathcare industry..

Stock exchange listing

In late 2005, China Construction Bank made an initial public offering on the Hong Kong Stock Exchange (SEHK:0939). Since its listing, the share price has risen about 50% (since Feb 2006). In late 2007, it made China's second-largest initial public offering of 57.12 billion Renminbi yuan (US$7.6 billion) on the Shanghai Stock Exchange (SSE:601939).

Source (edited): "http://en.wikipedia.org/wiki/China_Construction_Bank"

China Development Bank

The **China Development Bank (CDB)** (simplified Chinese: 国家开发银行; traditional Chinese: 國家開發銀行; pinyin: *Guójiā Kāifā Yínháng*) is a financial institution in the People's Republic of China (PRC) under the direct jurisdiction of the State Council. It is the only bank in China whose governor is a full minister. It is one of the three policy banks of the PRC, primarily responsible for raising funding for large infrastructure projects, including most of the funding for the Three Gorges Dam and Shanghai Pudong International Airport. The bank was established by the Policy Banks Law of 1994. The bank is described as the engine that powers the national government's economic development policies.

Debts issued by CDB are fully guaranteed by the central government of the People's Republic of China. The bank is the second-biggest bond issuer in China after the Ministry of Finance in 2009, accounting for about a quarter of the country's yuan bonds. In that year, the bank also overtook Bank of China to be China's biggest foreign-currency lender.

CDB has about 3500 employees at the end of 2004, about 1000 of them work at the Beijing Headquarters and the rest are spread out in 32 branches throughout the country. The bank also has offices in various countries all over the world. The bank does not take private savings, and hence does not have thousands of local branches like other major banks in China do.

According to Michelle Chan-Fishel, program manager of the Green Investments Program at Friends of the Earth–US in San Francisco, CDB is the only Chinese bank to adopt its own environmental financing standards. She said: "Based on publicly available data, only one Chinese bank – China Development Bank – has adopted its own environmental financing standards.".

The China Development Bank under the supervision of the central government is tasked with the development of socialist market economic system and to propel China's concerted and sustainable economic and social development.

History

The China Development Bank Tower in Shanghai.

The China Development Bank was established in March 1994 to provide development oriented finance for government projects of national priority. It is under the direct jurisdiction of the State Council or the People's Central Government. At present, it has 35 branches and 1 representative offices across the country. The bank provides financing for national projects such as infrastructure, basic industries, energy and transportation.

The main objective as a state financial institution is to support the macroeconomic policies of the central government and to support national economic development and strategic structural changes in the economy.

In the last decade alone, China Development Bank has issued 1.6 trillion yuan in loans to more than 4000 projects involving infrastructure, communications, transportation and basic industries. The investments are spread out along the Yellow River and both to the south and north of the Yangtze River. Increasingly, China Development Bank is focusing on developing the western and northwest provinces in China. This could help reduce the growing economic disparity in the western provinces and revitalize the old industrial bases of northeast China.

Since 1998, the bank successfully reduced bad debts and returned to profits under Governor Chen Yuan. Chen was formerly the executive deputy governor of the PRC's central bank, The People's Bank of China. International financial standards and best practices were also introduced into the bank.

The bank also plays a major development role in alleviating infrastructure or energy bottleneck in the Chinese economy. In 2003 CDB had loan arrangements for or evaluated and underwritten a total of 460 national debt projects and issued 246.8 billion yuan of loans. This accounted for 41% of its total investment. CBD loans to "bottleneck" investments that the government gives priorities amounted to 91% of the total. It also issued accumulatively 357.5 billion yuan of loans to western areas and 174.2 billion yuan to old industrial bases in Northeast China. All these loans have substantially increased the economic growth and structural readjustments of the Chinese economy.

At the end of 2004, the bank's total credit assets amounted to RMB 1378.6 billion, with current principal and interest recovery ratio of 99.77%, the indicator having maintained world-class performance for 20 consecutive quarters. The bank's non-performing loan ratio stood at 1.21%, down a year-on-year 0.13 percentage points. The coverage ratio of its risk reserves against non-performing loans hit 285%, and; its capital adequacy ratio reached 10.51%. During 2004, the bank made a profit of about US $2 billion.

In year 2005 and 2006, China Development Bank successfully issued two pilot ABS products in domestic China market. Together with another ABS products issued by China Construction Bank, they have set the corner stone for a promising debt capital & structured finance market.

At the end of 2010, CDB had US$687.8 billion in loans, more than twice as much as the World Bank.

The China Development Bank will continue to play significant role in reshaping the economy of the People's Republic of China by providing crucial national investment in high priority sectors of the economy. They have a mandate to reduce economic bottlenecks in basic and pillar industries, infrastructure, energy, communications and other sectors. In other words, to alleviate and finally eliminate resource and supply restriction "bottlenecks" and institutional "bottlenecks" through development-oriented finance. This is hope to increase the competitiveness of the economy, increase economic growth and employment for millions of people. The bank also promotes the principle of "Five Aspects Coordination." In the process of financing, CDB aims to promote corporate governance structure, enterprise system as a legal entity, cash flow management and credit management culture.

Organizational structure

The Governor of the bank reports to the Board of Supervisors which is accountable to the central government. There are four vice governors and two assistant governors.

Specialized departments
- Policy Research
- Business Development
- Financial Research and Development Center
- Credit Risk Management
- Credit Administration
- Investment Banking
- International Finance
- Large Corporate Lending
- Project Appraisal (3)

General departments
- Treasury
- Supervision
- Personnel
- Auditing
- Education and Training
- Operating Center
- General Logistics
- Retired Staff
- Comprehensive Planning
- Accounting and Finance
- Legal

Management

Full profiles available here.
- **Governor** Chen Yuan, born January 1945. Graduated with a Masters degree in Industrial Economics from the Graduate School of Chinese Academy of Social Sciences.
- **Vice Governor** Yao Zhongmin, born June 1952. Graduated with a Masters degree in Investment Economics from Central South China University of Finance and Economics.
- **Vice Governor** Wang Yi, born April 1956. Graduated with a Doctorate in Economics from Southwest China University of Finance and Economics.
- **Vice Governor** Liu Kegu, born May 1947. Graduated with a Doctorate in Finance from Northeast China University of Finance and Economics.
- **Vice Governor** Gao Jian, born August 1949. Graduated with a Doctorate in Finance from the Institute of Financial Sciences of the Ministry of Finance.
- **Chief Compliance Officer** Li Changfu, born January 1945. Graduated with a Major in Machinery Manufacturing from Shandong Institute of Farm Machinery.
- **Assistant Governor** Zhao Jianping,

born in July 1953. Graduated with a Masters degree in International Corporate Management from the Management School of the University of Texas.
- **Assistant Governor** Xu Yiren, born January 1949. Graduated with a Masters degree in World Economics from the Central Party School.

Source (edited): "http://en.wikipedia.org/wiki/China_Development_Bank"

China Merchants Bank

Headquarters of China Merchants Bank in the West Futian district of Shenzhen

China Merchants Bank (CMB) (simplified Chinese: 招商银行; pinyin: *Zhāoshāng Yínháng* SEHK: 3968, SSE: 600036) is a bank headquartered in Shenzhen, China. Founded in 1987, it is the first share-holding commercial bank wholly owned by corporate legal entities.

CMB has over five hundred branches in mainland China and one in Hong Kong. In November 2007, as part of a drive for international growth, it won federal approval to open a branch in New York.

Business areas

CMB operates its businesses through personal banking business, including personal savings, personal loans, investment banking, foreign exchange trading, gold trading and bank card services, among others; corporate banking business, including corporate savings, corporate loans, international settlements, trade financing, assets custody, financing leasing services and corporate annuities, among others, as well as online banking services and electronic banking services.

As of December 31, 2008, the Bank had 44 branches and 623 sub-branches, one representative, one credit card center, one credit loan center for small companies, as well as 1,567 self-service banks in China.

Source (edited): "http://en.wikipedia.org/wiki/China_Merchants_Bank"

Chinese financial system

Beijing Financial Street, the economic centre of Beijing.

China's financial system is highly regulated and has recently begun to expand rapidly as monetary policy becomes integral to its overall economic policy. As a result, banks are becoming more important to China's economy by providing increasingly more finance to enterprises for investment, seeking deposits from the public to mop up excess liquidity, and lending money to the government.

As part of US$586 billion economic stimulus package of November 2008, the government plans to remove loan quotas and ceilings for all lenders, and increase bank credit for priority projects, including rural areas, small businesses, technology companies, iron and cement companies.

Financial reform

For the past few decades, the People's Bank of China has exercised the functions and powers of a central bank, as well as handling industrial and commercial credits and savings business; it was neither the central bank in the true sense, nor a commercial entity conforming to the law of the market economy. But since reform and opening-up began in 1978, China has carried out a series of significant reforms in its banking system, and strengthened its opening to the outside world. Consequently, the finance industry has made steady development. At the end of 2004, the balance of domestic and foreign currency savings deposits stood at 25,318.8 billion yuan and the balance of home and foreign currency loans came to 18,856.6 billion yuan. Now China has basically formed a financial system under the regulation, control and supervision of the central bank, with its state banks as the mainstay, featuring the separation of policy-related finance and commercial finance, the cooperation of various financial institutions with mutually complementary functions.

In 1984, the People's Bank of China stopped handling credit and savings business, and began formally to exercise central bank functions and powers by conducting macro-control and supervision over the nation's banking system. In 1994, the Industrial and Commercial Bank of China, the Bank of China, the Agricultural Bank of China and the China Construction Bank were transformed into state-owned commercial banks; and three policy-related banks were founded, namely, the Agricultural Development Bank of China, the National Development Bank and the China Import and Export Bank. In 1995, the Commercial Bank Law was promulgated, creating the conditions for forming the commercial bank system and organizational structure, and providing a legal basis for changing the specialized state banks to state-owned commercial banks.

Since 1996, the financial organizational system has gradually been improved; the wholly state-owned commercial banks have been transformed into modern financial enterprises handling currencies; over 120 shareholding medium and small-sized commercial banks have been set up or reorganized; and securities and insurance financial institutions have been further standardized and developed. April 2003 saw the formal establishment of the China Banking Regulatory Commission (CBRC). Since then, a financial regulatory system has been formed in which CBRC, China Securities Regulatory Commission (CSRC) and China Insurance Regulatory Commission (CIRC) work in coordination, each body having its own clearly defined responsibilities.

In January 2004, the State Council decided that the Bank of China and the China Construction Bank would start the experiment of transforming the shareholding system. The main tasks are to establish a standardized corporate governance and an internal system of rights and responsibilities in accordance with the requirements for modern commercial banks; to restructure the financial system, speed up the disposal of non-performing assets and to reinforce minimum capital requirement to build up first-class modern financial enterprises. Now, six shareholding commercial banks and urban commercial banks in China have begun to accept overseas investors as shareholders.

Opening up of the financial industry

Over the past 20-odd years, China's financial institutions in the Special Economic Zone, coastal open cities and inland central cities have approved a range of wholly foreign-owned and Chinese-foreign joint venture financial institutions. Every year since 2002, China has increased the number of cities where foreign banks are allowed to handle RMB business, and within five years such banks will be allowed to handle RMB business in any city. At the end of 2004, the total assets of foreign financial institutions in China reached over US$47 billion; foreign banks were allowed to handle RMB business in 16 areas, and 62 foreign banks from 19 countries and regions set up 191 business institutions in China, of which 116 were approved to handle RMB business. There were 211 foreign bank branches in China.

The CSRC has approved the establishment of 13 Sino-foreign equity joint venture fund management companies, and started to formally handle the application of establishment of joint venture fund management companies with a maximum 49 percent foreign share; the CIRC declared that: from December 11, 2004 on, foreign insurance companies could handle health insurance, group insurance, life insurance and annuity insurance businesses; regional restrictions on establishing wholly foreign-funded insurance institutions were canceled and the proportion of the foreign share in joint venture insurance agencies was allowed to reach 51 percent.

Foreign banks have expanded their China-related business scope. In November 2003, the CBRC started to implement new policies, e.g., permitting foreign banks to provide RMB services to all kinds of Chinese enterprises in areas with open RMB business (previously, these banks' RMB services were restricted to foreign-funded enterprises, foreigners and people from Hong Kong, Macao and Taiwan in cities with open RMB business). The new policy also encourages qualified international strategic investors to join the restructuring and reforming of China's banking and financial institutions on a voluntary and commercial basis.

Meanwhile, all China's commercial banks have set up branches overseas, and started an international credit business. The Bank of China ranks first in the number and scale of overseas outlets. In 1980, China resumed membership of the World Bank, and returned to the International Monetary Fund. In 1984, China started business contacts with the Bank for International Settlements. In 1985, China formally joined the African Development Bank and in 1986 formally became a member of the Asian Development Bank.

Economic reform

The ongoing development of China's financial system will play a critical role in the country's effort to narrow social disparities and pursue balanced growth. Reforming the financial system would increase the rate of GDP growth and help spread China's new wealth more evenly. If the reforms directed additional funds to private companies — China's new growth engine — the economy would generate significantly higher returns for the same level of investment and GDP would rise. Such a shift will stimulate mass job creation in the strongest areas of China's economy and increase tax revenues to finance social programs.

After more than a quarter century of reform and opening to the outside world, by 2005 China's economy had become the second largest in the world after the United States when measured on a purchasing power parity (PPP) basis. The government has a goal of quadrupling the gross domestic product (GDP) by 2020 and more than doubling the per capita GDP. Central planning has been curtailed, and widespread market mechanisms and a reduced government role have prevailed since 1978. The government fosters a dual economic structure that has evolved from a socialist, centrally planned economy to a socialist market economic system, or a "socialist market economy with Chinese characteristics". Industry is marked by increasing technological advancements and productivity. People's communes were eliminated by 1984 — after more than 25 years — and the system of township-collective-household production was introduced to the agricultural sector. Private ownership of production assets is legal, although some nonagricultural and industrial facilities are still state-owned and centrally planned. Restraints on international trade were relaxed when China acceded to the World Trade Organization in 2001. Joint ventures are encouraged, especially in the coastal Special Economic Zones and open coastal cities. A sign of the affluence that the reformed economy has brought to China might be seen in the number of its millionaires (measured in U.S. dollars): a reported 236,000 millionaires in 2004, an increase of 12 percent over two years earlier.

Chinese officials cite two major trends that have an effect on China's market economy and future development: world multipolarization and regional integration. In relation to these trends, they foresee the roles of China and the United States in world affairs and with one another as very important. Despite successes, China's leaders face a variety of challenges to the nation's future economic development. They have to maintain a high growth rate, deal effectively with the rural workforce, improve the financial system, continue to reform the state-owned enterprises, foster the productive private sector, establish a social security system, improve scientific and educational development, promote better international cooperation, and some believe, change the role of the government in the economic system. Despite constraints the international market has placed on China, it nevertheless became the world's third largest trading nation in 2004 after only the United States and Germany.

The Fifth Plenum of the Sixteenth CPC Central Committee took place in October 2005. The Fifth Plenum approved the new Eleventh Five-Year Plan (2006–10), which emphasizes a shift from extensive to intensive growth in order to meet demands for improved economic returns; the conservation of resources to include a 20% reduction in energy consumption by 2010; and an effort to raise profitability. Better coordination of urban and rural development and of development between nearby provincial regions also is emphasized in the new plan.

Government finances and budget

China's government debt is less than 25% of gross domestic product (about 22.10% in 2006). (See *List of countries by public debt*.)

China has a budget deficit of around 1.5% of GDP. China projected a budget deficit of 295 billion yuan in 2006, down 1.7% from 2005. The overall budget deficit in 2004 was approximately US$26 billion, an amount equivalent to about 1.5% of GDP. In 2007, economic planners expect China's already small budget deficit to shrink again. According to economists, this has afforded China to spend more on public services such as education and healthcare.

The government budget for 2004 was US$330.6 billion in revenue and US$356.8 billion in expenditures. 95.5% of revenue was from taxes and tariffs, 54.9% of which was collected by the central government and 45% by local government. The expenditures were for culture, education, science, and health care (18%); capital construction (12%); administration (14%); national defense (7.7%); agriculture, forestry, and water conservancy (5.9%); subsidies to compensate for price increases (2.7%); pensions and social welfare provisions (1.9%); promotion of innovation, science, and technology (4.3%); operating expenses of industry, transport, and commerce (1.2%); geological prospecting (0.4%), and other (31.9%).

Taxation

Before the reform and opening, China exercised a single taxation system. Because taxation had no connection with the economic activities of enterprises, this system lacked vitality. In 1981, the Chinese government began to collect income tax from Sino-foreign joint ventures and solely foreign-funded enterprises, taking the first step in taxation system reform. From 1983 to 1984, the reform consisting of the replacement of profits by taxes was carried out in domestic enterprises, and a foreign-related taxation system was set up. As a result, instead of a single tax category, a compound taxation system in which turnover and income taxes were the mainstay and other tax categories were in coordination with it was initially in place and promoted the control of finances and the economy. In 1994, the reform of the taxation system was deepened, and a complete structural adjustment of the taxation system was made by taking the market economy as the norm. In 1996, China lowered the rate of customs duties and export drawback, and exercised import supervision.

Inflation

China's annual rate of inflation averaged 6% per year during the 1990–2002 period. Although consumer prices declined by 0.8% in 2002, they increased by 1.2% in 2003. China's estimated inflation rate in 2006 was 1.8%.

Banking sector

China's banking system is highly regulated with six major banks, each having specific tasks and duties. The People's Bank of China is the largest bank in China and acts as the Treasury. It also issues currency, monitors money supply, regulates monetary organizations and formulates monetary policy for the

State Council. The Bank of China manages foreign exchange transactions and manages foreign exchange reserves. The China Development Bank distributes foreign capital from a variety of sources, and the China International Trust and Investment Corporation (CITIC) was previously a financial organization that smoothed the inflow of foreign funds, but is now a full bank, allowing to compete for foreign investment funds with the Bank of China. The China Construction Bank lends funds for capital construction projects from the state budget, and finally the Agricultural Bank of China functions as a lending and deposit taking institution for the agricultural sector.

Banking reform

Financial reform in China's banking sector include the introduction of leasing and insurance, and operational boundaries are being slowly eroded to promote competition for customers who are now permitted to choose banks as well as hold accounts in more than one bank.

Banking reform was initiated in China in 1994, and the Commercial Banking Law took effect in July 1995. The aims of these actions were to strengthen the role of the central bank—the People's Bank of China—and to allow private banks to be established. The People's Bank of China was established in 1948. It issues China's currency and implements the nation's monetary policies. China's oldest bank, founded in 1908, is the Bank of Communications Limited, a commercial enterprise located in Shanghai. China's second oldest bank was established in 1912 as the Bank of China. Since 2004 it has become a shareholding company known as the Bank of China Limited and handles foreign exchange and international financial settlements. The Agricultural Bank of China, founded in 1951, is mainly involved in rural financing and the provision of services to agricultural, industrial, commercial, and transportation enterprises in rural areas. Other major banks include the China Construction Bank; established in 1954 as the People's Construction Bank of China, it has been a state-owned commercial bank since 1994 and maintains some 15,400 business outlets inside and outside China, including six overseas branches and two overseas representative offices. The China Construction Bank was restructured in 2003 into a shareholding bank called the China Construction Bank Corporation, with the state holding the controlling shares. CITIC was founded in 1979 to assist economic and technological cooperation, finance, banking, investment, and trade. The Industrial and Commercial Bank of China was founded in 1984 to handle industrial and commercial credits and international business. The Agricultural Development Bank of China, Export and Import Bank of China, and State Development Bank all were founded in 1994. China's first private commercial national bank, the China Minsheng Banking Corporation, was opened in 1996. Commercial banks are supervised by the China Banking Regulatory Commission, which was established in 2003. In 2005 the commission announced the launching of a new postal savings bank to replace the old system and its more than 36,000 outdated outlets nationwide.

Foreign banks

Since the inception of the "open door policy", a number of foreign banks have been permitted to open their doors in major cities in China. However, these are largely representative branches, with only a few being permitted to carry out branch functions in Shanghai and Shenzhen. Their participation in China's financial system has been limited, but as China starts to borrow more from abroad, their role may become greater in the future.

When first permitted in the mid-1980s, foreign banks were restricted to designated cities and could deal only with transactions by foreign companies in China. After those restrictions were loosened following China's accession to the World Trade Organization in 2001, some foreign banks have been allowed to provide services to local residents and businesses. In 2004 there were some 70 foreign banks with more than 150 branches in China. In 2007 a limited number of foreign banks were allowed to issue debit cards in China (and Bank of East Asia was allowed to issue a credit card). This made banking with a foreign bank more convenient, as money in accounts could be accessed at ATMs like customers of local banks could. In 2009 this number grew to six, but only two of these are not tied to Hong Kong.

Stock exchanges

There are stock exchanges in Beijing, Shanghai (the third largest in the world), and Shenzhen and futures exchanges in Shanghai, Dalian, and Zhengzhou. They are regulated by the China Securities Regulatory Commission.

Stock market

In 1990 and 1991, China set up stock exchanges in Shanghai and Shenzhen. In the past decade, the Chinese stock market has completed a journey that took many countries over a century to cover; China's stock market today has capital approaching 3,705.6 billion yuan, 1,377 listed companies and 72.16 million investors.

The Chinese stock market has promoted the reform of government-owned corporations and the change of their systems, and enabled a stable transition between the two systems. On the strength of the stock market in the past decade, many large state-owned enterprises have realized system change.

The change also has stimulated medium and small-sized state-owned enterprises to adopt the shareholding system, thus solving the most important issue - the system problem - during the transition from planned to a market economy. As for ordinary citizens, bank deposit is not the only way to put their money, the stock market has become one of the most important channels for investment.

Methods of stock trading are constantly being improved. Today, a network system for securities exchange and account settlement has been formed, with the Shanghai and Shenzhen exchanges as the powerhouse, radiating to all parts of the country. In 2004, China issued 123 kinds of A share, and 23 rights issues, collecting a total of 83.6 billion yuan; and 28 kinds of B and H shares, collecting a total of 67.5 billion yuan.

Development

As China's economy becomes more integrated with the rest of the world its financial system will become more in line with international practices.

China has also learnt from Hong Kong's financial system, with the help of the Hong Kong Monetary Authority.

Trade balance

China had a favorable balance of trade of US$32 billion in 2004 and US$38.7 billion in 2003. These amounts reflect the general course of a favorable trade balance during the previous eight years. In 1996 China's trade balance was US$12.2 billion, peaking at US$43.4 billion in 1998 but declining to US$24.1 billion by 2000 before starting its new increase.

Balance of payments

China's current account balance in 2004 was nearly US$68.7 billion. Added to this total was US$54.9 billion in foreign direct investment (exceeding that invested in the United States). When other investments, assets, and liabilities are brought into the calculation, the overall balance of payments was US$206.1 billion in 2004, compared with US$75.2 billion in 2002 and US$116.5 billion in 2003.

External debt

According to United Nations statistics for 2001, China's external and public, or publicly guaranteed, long-term debt had reached US$91.7 billion. China's debt had grown steadily during the 1990s, peaked at US$112.8 billion in 1997, and then declined annually thereafter. By 2004 China had US$618.5 billion in its international reserve account, 98.6 percent of which was from foreign exchange, not including the Bank of China's foreign exchange holdings.

Foreign aid and foreign investment

China is the recipient of bilateral and multilateral official development assistance and official aid to individual recipients. In 2003 it received US$1.3 billion in such disbursements, or about US$1 per capita. This total was down from the 1999 figures of US$2.4 billion and US$1.90 per capita. Some of this aid comes to China in the form of socioeconomic development assistance through the United Nations (UN) system. China received US$112 million in such UN assistance annually in 2001 and 2002, the largest portion coming from the UN Development Programme (UNDP).

China also obtains foreign capital through foreign loans, foreign direct investment (FDI), and other investment by foreign businesses. Since 1980 foreign businesses from more than 170 countries and regions have invested in Chinese joint-venture enterprises. Most joint-venture activities are located in coastal cities and increasing numbers in inland cities as well. Some 300 of the 500 top transnational companies in the world have invested in China, and foreign investments have become an important capital source for China's economic development. In 1999 FDI totaled US$40.3 billion. Between 1979 and 1999, cumulative FDI totaled US$305.9 billion, US$40.3 billion of which was invested in 1999 alone. In that year, China had approved the establishment of 342,000 foreign-funded enterprises, more than 100,000 of which have gone into operation. Contracted FDI reached nearly US$82.8 billion in 2002, US$115 billion in 2003, US$153.48 in 2004, and US$130.33 billion in the first nine months of 2005.

In 2007, China enacted a new law for corporate income tax which would unify the rates paid by foreign and domestic firms at 25 percent. Domestic firms used to pay 33 percent and foreign-funded firms 15 percent. Analysts say the overall impact on foreign direct investment would be limited due to China's relatively cheap labor and the promise of a huge market.

Currency and foreign exchange control

China's currency is the renminbi (RMB, "people's currency") or yuan. The interbank exchange rate on August 1, 2006, was US$1 = RMB7.98. The RMB is made up of 100 fen or 10 jiao. Coins are issued in denominations of one, two, and five fen; one and five jiao, and one RMB. Banknotes are issued in denominations of one, two, and five jiao; and one, two, five, 10, 50, and 100 RMB.

The Renminbi is issued and controlled solely by the People's Bank of China. RMB exchange rates are decided by the People's Bank of China and issued by the State Administration of Foreign Exchange, the latter exercising the functions and powers of exchange control.

In 1994, China reformed the foreign exchange system, combined the RMB exchange rates, adopted the bank exchange settlement system and set up a unified inter-bank foreign exchange market. On this basis, China included the foreign exchange business of the foreign-invested enterprises in the bank's exchange settlement system in 1996. On December 1, 1996, China formally accepted Article 8 of the Agreement on International Currencies and Funds, and realized RMB convertibility under the current account ahead of schedule. Meanwhile, China has been active in promoting bilateral currency exchange between ASEAN and China, Japan and the Republic of Korea (10+3). At the end of 2004, China's foreign exchange reserves reached US$609.9 billion and its share in the International Monetary Fund has risen from 11th to 8th place. The variety of financial businesses has been increasing steadily, and China has opened an array of new businesses to become integrated into the various aspects of modern international financial business, such as consumer credit, securities investment funds and insurance-linked investments.

Fiscal year

China's fiscal year follows the calendar year (January 1 to December 31).

Insurance

China's insurance industry started to recover in 1980, after a 20 year standstill. In 1981, the People's Insurance Company of China was transformed from a government department into a specialized company, with branches or sub-branches in every part of China. 1988 witnessed the founding of the Ping An Insurance (Group) Company of China and the Pacific Insurance Company, both mainly active in the coastal areas. In 1996, the People's Insurance Company of China made a big step forward in transforming its administration and operational mode, in setting up a modern enterprise system, and integrating with the international market. The Insurance Law of 1985 and the founding of the China Insurance Regulatory Commission in 1988 provided the legal basis and specific rules for the operation of the insurance market. In 1980, China only had one insurance company; by 2004 there were 62, with a total revenue of premiums of 431.8 billion yuan, of which 100.4 billion were paid as compensation and payment.

Source (edited): "http://en.wikipedia.org/wiki/Chinese_financial_system"

Citibank (China)

Citibank (China) Company Limited (simplified Chinese: 花旗银行(中国)有限公司) was one of the first foreign banks to incorporate locally in mainland China in 2007. The Chinese unit of Citibank has been operating since 1902 and became the first American bank to establish operations in China. An office tower, the Citigroup Tower, in Lujiazui, Shanghai is named after the bank.

The China Banking Regulatory Commission announced on 24 December 2006 its approval for foreign banks to start their preparatory work for setting up local incorporations in mainland China. Citibank was one of nine foreign banks to have applied for the incorporation. Its subsidiary Citibank (China) was founded in 1 April 2007, and it started operations in 2 April.

Company Profile

Citibank China has come a long way since 2000, when the highly restricted banking sector just barely allowed it to exist. Today, Citibank has a growing presence along the North-East and South-East of China, with a total of 25 consumer bank outlets in the eight provinces of Shanghai, Beijing, Guangzhou, Shenzhen, Chengdu, Tianjin, Hangzhou and Dalian. In its attempt to spread its influence across the country, Citibank has been more inclined to mergers and acquisitions than joint ventures. In 2007, Citibank China saw its operating income double to RMB 2.2 billion Yuan and its net income reach RMB 665 million. In addition, it is one of only five non-Chinese banks that can locally issue UnionPay debit cards. It also issues credit cards in partnership with Shanghai Pudong Development Bank.

Source (edited): "http://en.wikipedia.org/wiki/Citibank_(China)"

County Bank

A **County Bank** is a kind of financial institution with the purpose of boosting rural economic development, which has developed in China since 2005.

In 2007, China Banking Regulatory Commission promulgated "The Temporary Rule of County Bank", in which the establishment process, organization and structure, as well as business scope of a county bank are specified.

Afterwards, CBRC further published two rules with detailed requirements on county banks, namely "Notice on Printing and Distributing the Guidelines for Examination and Approval of the Establishment of County Banks" and "Notice on the Relevant Policies for County Banks, Loan Companies, Rural Mutual Cooperatives and Small Loan Companies".

Up to October 31, 2008, there are 62 county banks opened in China according to CBRC's report.

Source (edited): "http://en.wikipedia.org/wiki/County_Bank"

Exim Bank of China

The Export-Import Bank of China (China Exim Bank) (simplified Chinese: 中国进出口银行; traditional Chinese: 中國進出口銀行; pinyin: *Zhōngguó Jìnchūkǒu Yínháng*) is one of three institutional banks in China which chartered to implement the state policies in industry, foreign trade, diplomacy, economy and finance to provide policy financial support so as to promote the export of Chinese products and services. It was founded in 1994, and is subordinated to the State Council.

China Eximbank does not publish figures for overseas loans. However, U.S. officials estimate that it finances more than the total export financing of the Group of Seven industrialized nations combined. The *Financial Times* estimates that in 2009 and 2010, China Eximbank and China Development Bank (CDB) together signed loans of at least $110 billion to other developing country governments and companies, more than the World Bank over a similar period.

China Eximbank does not abide by

export financing guidelines promulgated by the OECD, sparking criticism from competing export nations. According to U.S. Export-Import Bank Chairman Fred Hochberg, "They're winning deals in part because they're not playing by the rules."

Organizational structure

Internal Departments
- Executive Office
- Human Resources Department
- Business Development & Innovation Department
- Corporate Business Department
- Shipping Financing Department
- Onlending Department
- Planning & Financial Management Department
- Evaluation Department
- Auditing Department
- Legal Affairs Department
- International Business Department
- Risk Management Department
- Administrative Department
- Supervision Office
- Economic Research Department
- Department of Special Account Financing
- Corporate Business Department
- Concessional Loan Department
- Treasury Department
- Information Technology Department
- Compliance Department
- Accounting Department
- Workers Union
- Software Development Department
- Party & League Affairs Department

Business Branches
- Shanghai Branch
- Shenzhen Branch
- Nanjing Branch
- Dalian Branch
- Chengdu Branch
- Qingdao Branch
- Zhejiang Branch
- Hunan Branch
- Chongqing Branch
- Xi'an Branch

Source (edited): "http://en.wikipedia.org/wiki/Exim_Bank_of_China"

China Guangfa Bank

China Guangfa Bank (simplified Chinese: 广发银行; traditional Chinese: 廣發銀行; pinyin: *Guǎng Fā Yínháng*, abbr: **CGB**), previously **Guangdong Development Bank** (simplified Chinese: 广东发展银行; traditional Chinese: 廣東發展銀行; pinyin: *Guǎngdōng Fāzhǎn Yínháng*), is a bank based in Guangzhou, Guangdong in People's Republic of China. The bank was established in September 1988 as a joint stock commercial bank.

The bank established its first "overseas" branch in the then Portuguese-administered Macau in 1993, and its registered name is Banco de Desenvolvimento de Cantão, Sucursal de Macau (廣東發展銀行澳門分行).

China Guangfa Bank is a mid-size national bank with more than 500 branches in China. Based in the Guangdong province bordering Hong Kong, GDB has assets of $47.9 billion, 12 million consumer customers, 9 million bank cardholders, 16,000 small and medium-sized business customers and 12,474 employees. Its problems seem to lie in weak capitalization and a history of bad loans.

Citigroup has a 20% stake, while IBM holds 4.74%, keeping the two American companies below the 25% threshold for overall foreign ownership. China Life and State Grid each owns 20%, CITIC Trust, 12.85% and Puhua will hold the remaining 8% of the equity sold.

Source (edited): "http://en.wikipedia.org/wiki/China_Guangfa_Bank"

HSBC Bank (China)

HSBC Bank (China) Company Limited (simplified Chinese: 汇丰银行(中国)有限公司; often abbreviated as 汇丰中国) was one of the first foreign banks to incorporate locally in mainland China in 2007. It is part of the worldwide HSBC Group and is wholly owned by Hong Kong-based The Hongkong and Shanghai Banking Corporation Limited.

Chinese banking

In mainland China, HSBC has the largest services network among foreign banks. The bank offers a full range of services that cater to both middle-class individuals and to business-oriented individuals as well, from a robust network of 37 main branches, and 23 smaller branches.

HSBC having invested over USD5 billion in select mainland financial services entities and in the growth of its own operations, including a 19.90% stake in Bank of Communications, a 16.8% stake in Ping An Insurance, and an 8% stake in Bank of Shanghai.

History

The Hongkong and Shanghai Banking Corporation established its Shanghai branch office on 3 April 1865, previous to other upstarts of HSBC, and indeed, as part of the historic English investment of Eastern Asian nations in the 19th century. Apart from the period 1941–1945, during which Japan forced HSBC and other foreign-invested banks to leave the local market, it has had a continuous presence in the city. HSBC was historically housed in one of the largest and most impressive buildings on The Bund, Shanghai's boulevard formerly known as the "Wall Street of the Orient". In April 1955, HSBC handed over this office to the Communist government, and its activities were continued in rented premises. Its activities were mainly in inward remittances and export bills until the economic reforms of the late 1970s. Chinese authorities had offered to lease HSBC its old headquarters on The Bund in 1995 but the offer was turned down. In 2000, HSBC China moved into HSBC Tower across the river in the Pudong area of Shanghai. In 2010, HSBC China's headquarters moved out of the HSBC Tower and moved into HSBC Building in Shanghai IFC.

Local incorporation

The China Banking Regulatory Commission announced on 24 December 2006 its approval for foreign banks to start their preparatory work for setting up local incorporations in mainland China. These foreign banks can launch the RMB retail business of below RMB1 million for Chinese domestic citizens after the inspection and confirmation by the relevant banking regulatory administration authorities. The Hongkong and Shanghai Banking Corporation was one of nine foreign banks to have applied for the incorporation. In 1 April 2007, the mainland China offices of The Hongkong and Shanghai Banking Corporation transferred to its subsidiary HSBC Bank (China), and it started operations in 2 April. The registered capital and paid-up capital of HSBC Bank (China) is equivalent to RMB8 billion. However, The Hongkong and Shanghai Banking Corporation still has a branch in Shanghai, which conducts foreign currency wholesale banking business.

Source (edited): "http://en.wikipedia.org/wiki/HSBC_Bank_(China)"

Harbin Bank

Harbin Bank (in Chinese: 哈尔滨银行) is a commercial bank, with its headquarters in Harbin, Heilongjiang Province, China. It was established in 1997 as Harbin City Commercial Bank, opened its branches in Harbin City only, but changed its name to Harbin Bank in 2007 and has since opened branches in Dalian, Tianjin Shuangyashan and Jixi.

Harbin Banks in the past

In 1921, Harbin Bank was established, which later was merged with Central Bank of Manchou.

Separately, the Harbin Bank was also established in 1944 through a merger of Detai and Dacheng Banks, whose stock was 36 percent owned by the Japanese Government and the Central Bank of Manchou, which was requisitioned by the People's Republic of China government in 1954.

Source (edited): "http://en.wikipedia.org/wiki/Harbin_Bank"

Hua Xia Bank

Hua Xia Bank (simplified Chinese: 华夏银行) (SSE: 600015) is a state-controlled publicly traded bank in the People's Republic of China. It is based in Beijing and was founded in 1992. Germany's Deutsche Bank holds 19.99% of the bank's shares as of 2010.

Source (edited): "http://en.wikipedia.org/wiki/Hua_Xia_Bank"

Industrial Bank (China)

Industrial Bank (SSE: 601166) was the old short name that was more commonly used in China from June 2001 until March 3, 2003 for **Industrial Bank Co.**

The former **Fujian Industrial Bank** (福建兴业银行) was established on August 26, 1988, and had its first name change in June 2001, renaming itself as **Fujian Industrial Bank Joint-Stock Corporation, Limited** (福建兴业银行股份有限公司), but the name was long and the bank was referred by others in China simply as **Industrial Bank** (simplified Chinese: 兴业银行; traditional Chinese: 興業銀行; pinyin: *Xīngyè Yínháng*) instead.

The bank had yet another name change on March 3, 2003 to finally settle for its current name **Industrial Bank Joint-Stock Corporation, Limited** (兴业银行股份有限公司), or more commonly known as **Industrial Bank Co.**

Source (edited): "http://en.wikipedia.org/wiki/Industrial_Bank_(China)"

Industrial Bank Co.

Industrial Bank Co., Ltd. SSE: 601166 (simplified Chinese: 兴业银行; traditional Chinese: 興業銀行; pinyin: *Xīngyè Yínháng*) is a bank based in Fuzhou, Fujian, China.

History

From the day of its establishment on 26 August 1988 to its first name change in June 2001, the bank was called **Fujian Industrial Bank** (Chinese: 福建兴业银行). From June 2001 to 3 March 2003, it was formerly known as **Fujian Industrial Bank Joint-Stock Corporation, Limited** (福建兴业银行股份有限公司), or abbreviated to **Industrial**

Bank (China).

The bank is one of China's joint-stock commercial banks. According to *The Banker*, the bank was ranked No. 210 among the top 1,000 banks worldwide 2005 in terms of total assets.

It should not be confused with the Industrial Bank of China, a defunct bank in the 1910s or the National Industrial Bank of China, which merged with the Bank of China in the 1950s nor with the Industrial and Commercial Bank of China (ICBC).

Main Business

The main business activities of the bank are:

Personal Banking
- deposits taking
- provision of loans
- local and international payments and settlements
- safe-box service
- credit cards

Corporate Banking
- bills acceptance and discounting
- issuing of financial bonds
- provision of letters of credit and guarantee facilities;
- agency collections and payments; agency sales of insurance
- bank card business

Institutional Banking
- agency issuing, cashing and underwriting of government bonds
- purchase and sales of government bonds and financial bonds
- inter-bank placements and borrowings services
- agency service in trading of foreign currencies
- settlements and sales of foreign currencies

Ownership Structure

As of 5 February 2007, the top ten shareholders in the bank were:
Source (edited): "http://en.wikipedia.org/wiki/Industrial_Bank_Co."

Industrial and Commercial Bank of China

Business Center in Tianjin

Industrial and Commercial Bank of China Ltd. (ICBC) (simplified Chinese: 中国工商银行; traditional Chinese: 中國工商銀行; pinyin: *Zhōngguó Gōngshāng Yínháng*, more commonly just 工行 Gōngháng) is the largest Bank of China's 'Big Four' state-owned commercial banks (the other three being the Bank of China, Agricultural Bank of China, and China Construction Bank). It was founded as a limited company on January 1, 1984. As of March 2010, it had assets of RMB 12.55 trillion (US$1.9 trillion), with over 18,000 outlets including 106 overseas branches and agents globally. In 2011, it ranked number 7 on Forbes Global 2000 list of worlds biggest public companies.

2005

The bank's Hong Kong operations are listed under the name ICBC Asia. It has purchased the Hong Kong subsidiary of Fortis Bank and rebranded it under its own name on 10 October 2005.

2006

In the runup to its planned initial public offering, on 28 April 2006, three "strategic investors" injected US$3.7 billion into ICBC :
- Goldman Sachs purchased a 5.75% stake for US$2.6 billion, the largest sum Goldman Sachs has ever invested-
- Dresdner Bank (a wholly owned subsidiary of Commerzbank) invested US$1 billion.
- American Express invested US$200 million.

World's largest IPO

The ICBC building in Xi'an

ICBC was simultaneously listed on both the Hong Kong Stock Exchange and Shanghai Stock Exchange on 27 October 2006. It was the world's largest IPO at that time valued at US$21.9 billion, surpassing the previous record US$18.4 billion IPO by Japan's NTT DoCoMo in 1998. In 2010, AgBank broke ICBC's IPO record when it raised $22.1 billion. China's largest commercial bank was also the first company to debut simultaneously on both the Hong Kong and Shanghai stock exchanges.

ICBC raised at least US$14 billion

in Hong Kong (H-shares) and another US$5.1 billion in Shanghai (A-shares). Due to heavy subscriptions, the greenshoe (i.e. over-allotment) placements were exercised and ICBC's take rose to US$21.9 billion (17% of ICBC's market value before the IPO), divided in US$16 billion in Hong Kong and US$5.9 billion in Shanghai. Following the global offering, the free float of shares was 22.14% of the market capitalization.

At the end of its first day of trading, the bank's shares closed up almost 15% at HK$3.52 in Hong Kong, compared with the listing price of HK$3.07, which was set at the top of the indicative range due to the strong demand. According to Bloomberg, ICBC's market capitalisation at the end of trade based on its Hong Kong shares was US$156.3 billion, making its equity the world's fifth highest among banks, just behind JPMorgan Chase. Meanwhile, ICBC's Shanghai-listed A-shares recorded more modest gains and ended up 5.1% from the offering price of RMB 3.12.

2008

In August 2008, ICBC became the second Chinese bank since 1991 to gain federal approval to establish a branch in New York City.

At the *2008 ALB China Law Awards*, ICBC was crowned:
- In-House of the Year - Banking & Financial Services In-House Team of the Year
- In-House of the Year - China In-House Team of the Year

2010

In 2010, ICBC loaned $400 million towards the completion of the Gibe III dam in Ethiopia. Groups that oppose the dam such as International Rivers and Survival International have complained about or have written to ICBC against the dam's funding.

Basic figures

As of 2006, ICBC has 2.5 million corporate customers and 150 million individual customers. In 2005, net profit was up 12.4% to RMB 33.7 billion, and the total loan balance was RMB 3,289.5 billion. Total liabilities are RMB 6,196.2 billion, up 11.2%. Delinquent or non-performing loans (NPL) total RMB 154.4 billion, a significant reduction although the figures are widely regarded as being somewhat higher than officially stated. It has an NPL ratio of 4.69% and a capital adequacy ratio of 9.89%.

As of June 29, 2009, ICBC is ranked the 17th largest bank in the world by assets and 8th in the world by tier 1 capital. In July 2007 it was ranked 30th in the world in terms of revenue.

Loans by industry

In millions of Chinese RMB (Yuan) in 2005:
- Manufacturing: 662,376, 20.1% (28.7% in 2004)
- Transportation, storage, postage & telecommunications: 367,371, 11.2% (10.2% in 2004)
- Power, gas and water: 281,179, 8.6% (7.0% in 2004)
- Retail and wholesale, catering: 265,906, 8.1% (6.9% in 2004)
- Property development: 194,024, 5.9%, (5.6% in 2004)
- Social service organization: 103,070, 3.1%, (3.2% in 2004)
- Construction: 89,666, 2.7%, (2.1% in 2004)
- Other industries: 313,804, 9.5%, (12.1% in 2004)
- Discounted bills: 392,717, 11.9%, (8.4% in 2004)
- Personal loans: 515,042, 15.7%, (13.1% in 2004)
- Overseas business:104,398, 3.2%, (2.7% in 2004)

Total: 3,289,553

Loan collateral

- Secured by mortgages: 34.1%
- Secured by other collateral: 22.1%
- Guaranteed loans: 23.3%
- Unsecured loans: 20.5%

Non-performing loans

At the end of 2004, 19.1% of ICBC's portfolio consisted of non-performing loans. In order to clean up ICBC's balance sheet and prepare it for overseas listing, the Chinese government orchestrated a series of capital injections, asset transfers, and government-subsidised bad loan disposals that eventually cost more than US$162 billion. This included an approval for a cash injection of US$15 billion (financed from China's massive foreign exchange reserves) on 28 April 2005. The Beijing-based state company, China Huarong, helped ICBC dispose of its bad loans. As the 2005 annual report records, just under 5% of loans are classified as non-performing, in comparison with the majority of western banks who have lower NPL ratios (US commercial banks around 1%).
Source (edited): "http://en.wikipedia.org/wiki/Industrial_and_Commercial_Bank_of_China"

Minsheng Banking Corp

China Minsheng Bank (simplified Chinese: 中国民生银行; traditional Chinese: 中國民生銀行; pinyin: *Zhōngguó Mínshēng Yínháng*) (SSE: 600016, SEHK: 1988), founded on January 12, 1996 in Beijing, is the first bank in China to be owned mostly by non-government enterprises. The bank was founded by Jing Shuping, a Chinese lawyer and businessman who become prominent in the People's Republic of China after the nation's founding in 1949.

Minsheng Bank has over two hundred banking outlets throughout China and relationships with more than seven hundred banks overseas. The bank was publicly listed on the Hong Kong Stock Exchange in 2009.
Source (edited): "http://en.wikipedia.org/wiki/Minsheng_Banking_Corp"

People's Bank of China

The **People's Bank of China** (**PBC** or **PBOC**) is the central bank of the People's Republic of China with the power to control monetary policy and regulate financial institutions in mainland China. The People's Bank of China has more financial assets than any other single public finance institution in world history.

History

The bank was established on December 1, 1948 based on the consolidation of the Huabei Bank, the Beihai Bank and the Xibei Farmer Bank. The headquarters was first located in Shijiazhuang, Hebei, and then moved to Beijing in 1949. Between 1949 and 1978 the PBC was the only bank in the People's Republic of China and was responsible for both central banking and commercial banking operations.

In the 1980s, as part of economic reform, the commercial banking functions of the PBC were split off into four independent but state-owned banks and in 1983, the State Council promulgated that the PBC would function as the central bank of China. Mr. Chen Yuan was instrumental in modernizing the bank in the early 1990's. Its central bank status was legally confirmed on March 18, 1995 by the 3rd Plenum of the 8th National People's Congress. In 1998, the PBC underwent a major restructuring. All provincial and local branches were abolished, and the PBC opened nine regional branches, whose boundaries did not correspond to local administrative boundaries. In 2003, the Standing Committee of the Tenth National People's Congress approved an amendment law for strengthening the role of PBC in the making and implementation of monetary policy for safeguarding the overall financial stability and provision of financial services.

Management

The top management of the PBC is composed of the governor and a certain number of deputy governors. The governor of the PBC is appointed into or removed from office by the President of the People's Republic of China. The candidate for the governor of the PBC is nominated by the Premier of the State Council and approved by the National People's Congress. When the National People's Congress is in adjournment, the Standing Committee of the National People's Congress sanctions the candidacy for the governor of the PBC. The deputy governors of the PBC are appointed into or removed from office by the Premier of the State Council.

The PBC adopts a governor responsibility system under which the governor supervises the overall work of the PBC while the deputy governors provide assistance to the governor to fulfill his or her responsibility.

The current governor is Zhou Xiaochuan. Other high-ranking deputies include Wang Hongzhang, Hu Xiaolian, Liu Shiyu, Ma Delun, Yi Gang, Du Jinfu, Li Dongrong, Guo Qingping.

Structure

The PBC has established 9 regional branches respectively in Tianjin, Shenyang, Shanghai, Nanjing, Jinan, Wuhan, Guangzhou, Chengdu and Xi'an, 2 operations offices in Beijing and Chongqing, 303 municipal sub-branches and 1809 county-level sub-branches.

It has 6 overseas representative offices (PBC Representative Office for America, PBC Representative Office (London) for Europe, PBC Tokyo Representative Office, PBC Frankfurt Representative Office, PBC Representative Office for Africa, Liaison Office of the PBC in the Caribbean Development Bank).

The PBC consists of 18 functional departments (bureaus).
- General Administration Department
- Legal Affairs Department
- Monetary Policy Department
- Financial Market Department
- Financial Stability Bureau
- Financial Survey and Statistics Department
- Accounting and Treasury Department
- Payment System Department
- Technology Department
- Currency, Gold and Silver Bureau
- State Treasury Bureau
- International Department
- Internal Auditing Department
- Personnel Department
- Research Bureau
- Credit Information System Bureau
- Anti-Money Laundering Bureau (Security Bureau)
- Education Department of the CPC PBC Committee

The following enterprises and institutions are directly under the PBC.
- China Anti-Money Laundering Monitoring and Analysis Center
- PBC Graduate School
- China Financial Publishing House
- Financial News
- China National Clearing Center
- China Banknote Printing and Minting Corporation
- China Gold Coin Incorporation
- China Financial Computerization Corporation
- China Foreign Exchange Trade System

Microfinance

- Rural Credit Cooperatives

List of Governors

- Nan Hanchen (南汉辰): October 1949 – October 1954
- Cao Juru (曹菊如): October 1954 – October 1964
- Hu Lijiao (胡立教): October 1964–1966
- Chen Xiyu (陈希愈): May 1973 – January 1978
- Li Baohua (李葆华): January 1978 – April 1982
- Lü Peijian (吕培俭): April 1982 – March 1985
- Chen Muhua (陈慕华): March 1985 – April 1988
- Li Guixian (李贵鲜): April 1988 – July 1993
- Zhu Rongji (朱镕基): July 1993 – June 1995

- Dai Xianglong (戴相龙): June 1995 – December 2002
- Zhou Xiaochuan (周小川): December 2002 – present

Interest rates

Previously, interest rates set by the bank were always divisible by nine, instead of by 25 as in the rest of the world. However, it no longer applies, since the central bank started increasing the rates by 0,25 percentage points at a time.

The most recent rate hike was on 6 July 2011, taking benchmark 1-year rates up by 25 basis points to 6.56% while depo rates were also hiked by 25 basis points to 3.5%.

Source (edited): "http://en.wikipedia.org/wiki/People%27s_Bank_of_China"

Ping An Bank

Ping An Bank is a joint-stock commercial bank with its headquarters in Shenzhen. It primarily operates in Shenzhen, Shanghai and Fuzhou. As a subsidiary of Ping An Insurance (Group) Company of China, Ltd. ("Ping An", HKEx 2318, SSE 601318), the bank is one of the three main pillars of Ping An Group: insurance, banking and asset management.

Source (edited): "http://en.wikipedia.org/wiki/Ping_An_Bank"

Postal Savings Bank of China

Post office in Shanghai offering postal savings services

Postal Savings Bank of China (PSBC) (中国邮政储蓄银行) is a commercial retail bank, which provides basic financial services, especially to SMEs, rural and low income customers. PSBC has 40,000 branches covering all regions of China.

PSBC was set up with an initial capital of RMB20 billion in 2007 from the State Post Bureau. Today it has RMB1.5billion in deposits and the second largest number of branches, after the Agricultural Bank of China.

Duriing the Global Financial Crisis, the government took several measures to spread its national economic stimulus plan specifically to rural areas. This included using microfinance services provided by the Postal Savings Bank as a tool for national development and poverty reduction. The bank with its extremely broad reach also assists China's credit cooperatives in their microcredit schemes.

Source (edited): "http://en.wikipedia.org/wiki/Postal_Savings_Bank_of_China"

Shanghai Pudong Development Bank

Shanghai Pudong Development Bank Co. Ltd (SPDB), (SSE: 600000) incorporated on January 9, 1993 with the approval of the People's Bank of China (August 28, 1992), is a joint-stock commercial bank with its headquarters located in Shanghai.

Shanghai Pudong Development Bank issued a 400 million A-share offer on September 23, 1993 on the Shanghai Stock Exchange. It became the first shareholding commercial bank to list with both Central Bank and China Securities Regulatory Commission's approval since the enactment of "Commercial Bank Law" and "Securities Law". Thus, the registered capital reached RMB 2.41 billion. 320 million shares of the issue were listed on the Shanghai Stock Exchange on November 10, 1999 (stock code 600000).

Purpose

The purpose of SPDB is to provide financial services for the development of Pudong, building Shanghai into one of the great international financial hubs, and to contribute to the national economic development and social progress.

By the end of 2004, the bank's total assets reached RMB 455.53 billion. The outstanding balance of all deposits stood at RMB 395.38 billion and outstanding loans of RMB 310.9 billion. After-tax profits totaled RMB 1930 million.

Bank branches

SPD Bank in Wuhan

The bank has set up 30 branches and offices in Shanghai Branch, Hangzhou Branch, Ningbo Branch, Nanjing Branch, Beijing Branch, Wenzhou Sub-branch, Suzhou Branch, Chongqing Branch, Guangzhou Branch, Shenzhen

Branch, Kunming Branch, Wuhu Sub-branch, Tianjin Branch, Zhengzhou Branch, Dalian Branch, Jinan Branch, Chengdu Branch, Xi'an Branch, Shenyang Branch, Wuhan Branch, Qingdao Branch, Taiyuan Branch (source Company's Annual Report 2007)

Historical developments

The headquarters of SPDB at The Bund of Shanghai

In 2005, *Citigroup*, the world's largest financial services firm, expects to wrap up talks within months to raise its stake to nearly a fifth in China's Pudong Development Bank, a senior executive said. Citigroup wants to quadruple its stake in Pudong Bank to 19.9%.

Under an agreement forged in 2002, Citigroup already has the option to raise its stake to 24.9% by 2008. From its headquarters on Shanghai's historic Bund - the HSBC Building - Pudong Bank today commands 328 branches across the country.

China has made banking reform a priority, because it fears the sector's problems could jeopardize economic stability. It is urging banks, big and small, to find foreign investors and seek listings. Citigroup, which became the world's most valuable financial services firm through a series of big acquisitions, had been viewed as a potential player in any foreign investments in China. But it did not take an expected plunge with state-backed China Construction Bank, and watched as rival Bank of America agreed to pay $3 billion for 9% of the Chinese lender. Citigroup has made significant investments elsewhere in Asia, with a $2.7 billion purchase of KorAm Bank in South Korea.

Source (edited): "http://en.wikipedia.org/wiki/Shanghai_Pudong_Development_Bank"

Shengjing Bank

Shengjing Bank (in Chinese: 盛京银行) is a commercial bank, with its headquarters in Shenyang, Liaoning Province, China. It was established in 1996 as **Shenyang City Commercial Bank**, opened its branch in Shenyang City only, but changed its name to Shengjing Bank in 2007 and has since opened a branch in Tianjin.

Source (edited): "http://en.wikipedia.org/wiki/Shengjing_Bank"

Shenzhen City Commercial Bank

Shenzhen City Commercial Bank (simplified Chinese: 深圳市商业银行; traditional Chinese: 深圳市商業銀行; pinyin: *Shēnzhènshì Shāngyè Yínháng*) is a commercial bank based in Shenzhen in the People's Republic of China.

Source (edited): "http://en.wikipedia.org/wiki/Shenzhen_City_Commercial_Bank"

Shenzhen Development Bank

Shenzhen Development Bank Co., Ltd. SZSE: **000001** (simplified Chinese: 深圳发展银行; traditional Chinese: 深圳發展銀行; pinyin: *Shēnzhèn Fāzhǎn Yínháng*) is a bank based in Shenzhen, Guangdong, People's Republic of China. It is listed on the Shenzhen Stock Exchange.

Source (edited): "http://en.wikipedia.org/wiki/Shenzhen_Development_Bank"

Sili Bank

Established in September 12 2001,**Sili Bank** (Traditional Chinese: 實利銀行, Simplified Chinese: 实利银行 *Shili Yinhang*; Hangeul: 실리은행, *Silli Ŭnhaeng*; Kanji: 実利銀行) also known as the Korea 626 Shenyang Co. (Hangeul:626기술봉사소, Simplified Chinese: 朝鲜626技术服务所沈阳办事处) is a financial institution based in Chilbosan/Qibaoshan Hotel (Hanzi/Hanja: 七宝山饭店) in Shenyang, Liaoning, China, closely related to the government of North Korea.

The name "sili" (實利) means "true profit" in both Chinese and Korean.

Since October 8 2001, the webmail

provider began offering a limited electronic mail relay service to and from North Korea, where Internet access is limited. Along with Chesin.com, Sili Bank appears to be one of only two e-mail gateways to DPRK.

Sili Bank maintains dedicated servers in Pyongyang and Shenyang, between which e-mail transmissions are exchanged once every 10 minutes (when the service commenced, this was hourly).

In 2001, it was initially limited to those who want to exchange e-mails with trade companies or government agencies. As of May 10, 2003, the fee for sending an e-mail to North Korea from abroad, was 0.1 euros per kilobyte for up to 40 kilobytes, and 0.02 euros for each additional kilobyte in each e-mail transmission. The minimum charge per e-mail was 1 euro (for an e-mail having a size up to 10 kilobytes). Customers must first pre-register with Sili Bank with prepayment for estimated usage over a three-month period to the webmaster Li Mingchun (Hanzi: 李明春). Sili Bank only allows e-mail relay between registered users of the service.

Source (edited): "http://en.wikipedia.org/wiki/Sili_Bank"

Taizhou Commercial Bank

The Head office of Taizhou Commercial Bank

Taizhou City Commercial Bank (TZB; simplified Chinese 台州市商业银行) is a city commercial bank headquartered in Taizhou, Zhejiang Province - China.

The Bank was founded on March 13, 2003, by an amalgamation of eight local credit unions with a registered capital of RMB 300 million and is the first non-state-controlled city commercial bank in China. As of September 30, 2009, total assets amounted to RMB 30.209 billion, with 43 branches and more than 2000 employees.

The KPMG research study "China's City Commercial Bank: Opportunity knocks?" (2007) ranked TZCB on place 12 out of China's Top 100 city commercial banks. In 2008, TZCB was awarded with the 3rd place in the "Comprehensive competitiveness rank of national city commercial banks" by the Chinese finance magazine "The Banker".

Business areas

TZCB is focused on SME finance and also has a big micro lending operation. The bank was the first partner bank in the China Development Bank Microfinance Project starting in 2005.

In 2010 the bank opned branches in Zhoushan territory, Hangzhou territory and Wenzhou territory and started its village bank network.h

Source (edited): "http://en.wikipedia.org/wiki/Taizhou_Commercial_Bank"

Xiamen International Bank

Xiamen International Bank (XIB) (simplified Chinese: 厦门国际银行; traditional Chinese: 廈門國際銀行; pinyin: *Xiàmén Guójì Yínháng*) was established in August 1985 as the first joint venture bank in China with capital of RMB 1.069 billion.

Locations

XIB is based in Xiamen, Fujian Province, which also operates subsidiaries including Xiamen International Investment Limited (XIIL) in Hong Kong and Luso International Banking Limited (LIB) which runs 11 branches in Macau.

In Mainland China, XIB operates branches and multiple sub-branches in cities including Beijing, Shanghai, Fuzhou, Zhuhai, Xiamen, and a representative office in Quanzhou.

Shareholders

- Industrial and Commercial Bank of China (18.75%)
- Fujian Investment and Enterprise Holdings Corporation (12%)
- Xiamen C&D Corporation Limited (7.5%)
- Min Xin Holdings Limited (HKSE listed) (36.75%)
- Asian Development Bank (10%)
- Shinsei Bank Limited (from Japan) (10%)
- Sino Finance Group Company Limited (from U.S.A) (5%)

Source (edited): "http://en.wikipedia.org/wiki/Xiamen_International_Bank"

Zhejiang Tailong Commercial Bank

Zhejiang Tailong Commercial Bank (simplified Chinese: 浙江泰隆商业银行) is a small Chinese commercial bank in Taizhou, Zhejiang province, China. The bank has a relatively short history. It is comparatively well known in China because of its intensive public relations work in context with the SME finance supported by the government. Is this context it was termed as the Chinese Grameen Bank. This comparison is not accurate. Tailong Commerial Bank operates in one of the richest and economically most active regions in China and targets local business men and not women living below the poverty line like Grameen. Also Grameen bank and Tailong Commercial Bank use fundamentally different lending technologies. The most important difference is that the Chinese bank is purely operating in the commercial mode and does not receive or provide any form of subsidize to or from anyone, because the bank executives do not believe that they are a charity organization.

History

the bank was established in 1993. The bank had a very humble beginning as a credit union with an asset of only one million Renminbi Yuan and seven employees in two small rented rooms dated back on June 28, 1993. The bank has since gradually expanded and today, it has a total of nine branches in addition to its headquarter and ranked number two behind Taizhou City Commercial Bank among the biggest eleven local banks in the Luqiao Precinct of Taizhou, Zhejiang, with 21.9% of total local deposits, and 20.27% of total local loans by the end of 2006. On August 15, 2006, the status of the bank was upgraded from credit union to commercial bank, and thus was accordingly renamed as Zhejiang Tailong Commercial Bank (浙江泰隆商业银行) from its original name Taizhou City Tailong Urban Credit Union (台州市泰隆城市信用社).

Although the credit union was performing adequately in the first half decade since its birth, it was struggling in the fiercely competitive Chinese market. As a result the bank focusses its market strategy on small and mid-sized business.

Since its incept, the bank has provided over 60 billion CNY (around $ 8 billion) to its clientele, and over 90% of which are peasants. For its loans made to microbusiness which averages 51,000 CNY (around $ 6,400), over 90% of the customers are peasants turned entrepreneurs. One of the practice of the bank copied from its larger rival Taizhou City Commercial Bank is that the bank must adjust its opening hour to that of its client. For example, if a client is vendor close at 9:00 pm, then the bank must not close at anytime earlier than 9:00 pm because the vendor may need to go to the bank after she/he closes.

Business

The bank has focused on SME loans up to a size of RMB 5 million. Over 90% of loans made is less than one million CNY (around $ 125,000.

Since its clientele often lacks the assets required by larger banks when applying for a loan, the Zhejiang Tailong Commercial Bank developed a method similar to the American immigration system: sponsorship. Lending decisions are not primarily based on assets, but on third party (guarantor) and other soft information.

The number of loan officers is more than one third of the total staff, due to the labor intensive nature of SME business.

In addition to the work of loan officers, the banks also institute a strict policy of not making any new loans to customers who still have not completely paid back an earlier loan. As a result of these measures, the non-performing loans of the bank has never exceeded 0.9%, and mostly are kept at less than 0.83% range.

Source (edited): "http://en.wikipedia.org/wiki/Zhejiang_Tailong_Commercial_Bank"

David Shou-Yeh Wong

David Shou-Yeh Wong (Traditional Chinese: 王守業; Simplified Chinese: 王守业), is a Hong Kong billionaire, finance tycoon and philanthropist.

Introduction

A native of Ningbo, Zhejiang Province, David Wong founded and is the current President of the Dah Sing Bank Limited. Wong also invests in Mainland China, including the Chongqing Business Bank.

He is Chairman of Dah Sing Life Assurance Company Ltd. as well as Vice-president of the Hong Kong Institute of Bankers.

In 2008's Forbes Hong Kong's 40 Richest list, Wong was ranked as one of Hong Kong's top 40 billionaires (No.37).

Source (edited): "http://en.wikipedia.org/wiki/David_Shou-Yeh_Wong"

Fang Chengguo

FANG Chengguo (Traditional Chinese: 方誠國, Simplified Chinese: 方诚国), is a renowed Chinese senior banker, and the former governor/president of the Bank of Communications, the former vice-president of the Agricultural Bank of China.

Biography
Born in Zhenhai, Ningbo, Zhejiang Province in Dec 1943, Fang joined the Communist Party of China in Nov 1963.

Fang first worked as a clerk in the Shanghai Branch of the People's Bank of China. He was continuously promoted into the positions of deputy group leader (組長), group leader (組長), deputy director of the department (副處長).

Fang also worked in the Shanghai Branch of the Agricultural Bank of China, chronologically as the deputy director of the department (副處長), deputy director (副主任), director (主任), assistant for the governor of Shanghai Branch (分行助理), deputy governor of the Shanghai Branch (分行行長), and finally the governor of the branch. Then he was transferred to the headquarters of Agricultural Bank of China in Beijing, eventually promoted as the deputy governor of the Agricultural Bank of China.

Afterward, Fang worked in the Bank of Communications, first as its deputy governor, the deputy secretary (party position), and the member of the board. Then he became the governor of the Bank of Communications, the secretary-in-general, and the vice-president of the board.
Source (edited): "http://en.wikipedia.org/wiki/Fang_Chengguo"

H.J. Shen

Hsi-Jui Shen (May 5, 1902 in Shanghai, China – 1994 in San Francisco, CA) was the former head of the central bank of China, and the only chief manager of Chinese descent for the banking conglomerate HSBC (appointed in 1964). Shen was also among the first students of Chinese descent at Dartmouth College (class of 1928) and Harvard Business School.
Source (edited): "http://en.wikipedia.org/wiki/H.J._Shen"

H. H. Kung

K'ung Hsiang-hsi (Chinese: 孔祥熙; pinyin: *Kǒng Xiángxī*; Wade–Giles: K'ung Hsiang-hsi) (September 11, 1881 – August 16, 1967), often known as **Dr. H. H. Kung**, was a wealthy Chinese banker and politician in the early 20th century. He was highly influential in determining the economic policies of the KMT government in the 1930s and 1940s. He was known as the richest man in China at that time.

Biography

Early life
Hsiang-hsi Kung was born in Taigu, Jinzhong, Shanxi. He was educated in the United States. He received his Bachelor of Arts from Oberlin College, and a Master of Arts and Law Degree from Yale University.

After completing his education abroad, Kung returned to his home province of Shanxi. During the 1911 Xinhai Revolution, Kung mobilized forces in support of Yan Xishan, helping Yan to overthrow the authority of the Qing government in Shanxi. Yan was soon recognized as the military governor of Shanxi by Yuan Shikai, and effectively controlled Shanxi until 1949, when the Communists took control of mainland China. After 1911, Kung became one of Yan's most trusted advisors.

After the Xinhai Revolution, Kung helped to establish a complex of Christian schools in Taigu that was supported and affiliated with Kung's alma mater, Oberlin College. After establishing this school complex, Kung became its principle. Kung's influence on Yan's thinking from 1911 onward was significant, and was a major factor in Yan's subsequent determination to modernize Shanxi. The reforms that Yan subsequently conducted won Yan widespread acclaim, and Shanxi gained a reputation during the Warlord Era as being the "Model Province".

In 1922 Shanxi experienced a serious famine. Kung, as one of Yan's most trusted advisors at the time, worked closely with the American Red Cross and missionary organizations like American Mission Board and the China International Famine Relief Commission to deliver relief supplies and to improve Shanxi's infrastructure to make the delivery of relief easier. According to foreign members of the Famine Relief Commission, the collective efforts of all involved were successful in preventing what otherwise would have been an "appalling calamity", and by 1923 conditions in Shanxi returned to normal.

Minister in the Kuomintang government
Kung was an early supporter of Sun Yat-sen, and worked with Wang Jingwei before serving in the government of Chiang Kai-shek. Kung began his career in the government of the Republic of China as the Minister of Industry, holding this position from 1927-1928 in the Wuhan Nationalist Government, led by Wang Jingwei. After the fall of Wang's government, Kung served as the Minister of Industry and Commerce from 1928-1931 in the Nanking Nationalist Government, and later as the Minister of Finance, from 1933–1944. Kung later became the Governor of the Central Bank of China, from 1933–1945. In 1927 one of his first acts in government was to balance the national budget. To raise the capital required, Kung increased the taxes on cigarettes by

50%. Several Shanghai cigarette factories demonstrated against these taxes with shutdowns. Kung also threatened to increase the salt tax by 28%.

Kung joined the central executive committee of the Kuomintang (KMT) in 1931. He served as Premier of the Republic of China from 1 January 1938 – 20 November 1939. Kung then served as the Vice-Premier of the Executive Yuan, from 1935-1945. Dr. Kung served as China's Chief Delegate to the International Monetary & Financial Conference in 1944, where he signed the Bretton Woods Accord during the Bretton Woods Conference at the Mount Washington Hotel, New Hampshire, in the United States. This conference established the International Monetary Fund (IMF) and the International Bank for Reconstruction and Development (IBRD), which today is part of the World Bank Group.

After his move to the central government, Kung continued to advocate for good relations between Chiang Kai-shek and Yan Xishan. Yan's opposition to Chiang during the 1930 Central Plains War caused Yan to formally retire from all positions of leadership in Shanxi, and to flee to the Manchurian city of Dalian. Kung's tireless advocacy for Yan within the central government was successful, as Chiang allowed Yan to return to Shanxi in 1931. Chiang clearly recognized Yan as the de facto reler of Shanxi by 1934.

In 1934 Kung stated, in response to the American "nationalization of silver", that "We also would like to nationalize silver but for China this is impossible because our Government is hampered by extraterritorial treaties. We do not want the price to skyrocket, for silver is vital to our national life."

Diplomacy with Axis powers

Kung traveled to Germany in 1937, attempting to enlist German aid against the Empire of Japan.

In 1937 Kung and two other Chinese KMT officials visited Germany and were received by Adolf Hitler in June 13. Hitler told Kung that "I understand that people in China think the Soviet Union is their friend. But from our talk I understand that you, Herr Doktor, realize the danger of Communist doctrines." Kung also convinced Hitler to cancel a scheduled speech at a Nazi conference by the Japanese Emperor's brother. Kung said, "I was able to make Hitler understand that Japan wanted to dominate the world...I was able to make Hitler think twice before getting too close to Japan." While in Germany Kung stated his "deep satisfaction" with Hitler.

Hitler, Göring and Dr. Schacht bestowed upon Kung an honorary degree, and attempted to open China's market to German exports. Hitler, Goring, and Schacht earmarked for Chinese students 100,000 Reichsmarks for studying in Germany after they persuaded an industrialist to set aside the money for that purpose. Kung, in favor of commercial credits, refused an international loan offer by Hitler.

Kung also met Dr. Hjalmar Schacht while in Germany. Scherr told him that "German-Chinese friendship stemmed in good part from the hard struggle of both for independence." H .H. Kung said, "China considers Germany its best friend...I hope and wish that Germany will participate in supporting the further development of China, the opening up of its sources of raw materials, the upbuilding of its industries and means of transportation."

Kung also visited Roosevelt and Mussolini in 1937. Kung said "I thought Mussolini was doing great things for Italy... we got along well. I thought he would be a good ally of our Government."

During the Second Sino-Japanese War

By the time of the Second Sino Japanese War (1937–1945), Kung had achieved a reputation as an exceptionally powerful and manipulative figure within the Nationalist government. By the time that the KMT government moved to Chongqing, Kung was running his own secret service. The Communist Zhou Enlai, while serving as the CCP ambassador to Chongqing, was notably successful in gaining the confidence of Kung's advisor, Hu Egong, allowing Zhou to conduct his intelligence work more efficiently.

In January 1938, Kung, a 75th-generation descendant of Confucius, greeted his relative, Duke Kung Te-cheng, who was also a descendant of Confucius, after Kung Te-cheng had fled to Hankou after the Japanese invasion of Shandong. After Kung Te-cheng fled, the Japanese blew up his residence on Mount Tai. *TIME* magazine addressed Kung Te-cheng by the title "Duke Kung", and referred to his residence as the "ducal seat".

After a string of Japanese mishaps in 1938, Kung gave a radio address in which he stated that "God is helping China!" Kung's radio speech came after reports that a Japanese attempt to seize Hankou had failed and, that and constant Chinese guerilla activity had seized territory captured by Japan.

In 1944, Kung gave a speech at the China house with one of Mencius's direct descendants, Dr. Meng Chih. Both were alumni of American institutions.

After the retreat of the KMT to Taiwan at the end of the Chinese Civil War, he moved to the United States.

Personal life

Kung had a habit of smoking stogies (a type of cigar). TIME magazine claimed that Kung smoked "15 Havana cigars" a day. He was a Christian.

Kung was a 75th generation descendant of Confucius, as indicated by the generation name 祥 (Hsiang; pinyin: Xiáng). Kung's father was (Chinese: 孔繁慈; pinyin: *Kǒng Fáncí*; Wade–Giles: K'ung Fan-tsi) (1861 - 1911), a 74th generation descendant of Confucius, indicated by the generation name fan (繁).

Kung first married Han Yu-mei in 1910, but she died in 1913. In 1914 Kung married his second wife, Soong Ai-ling, the eldest of the Soong sisters. This marriage made Kung the brother-in-law of Soong Mei-ling, the wife of Chiang Kai-shek. The children of Kung and Soong were :
- Kung Ling-i (孔令儀), female
- Kung Ling-kan (孔令侃), male
- Kung Ling-chun (孔令俊), also known as Kung Ling-wei (孔令偉), female
- Kung Ling-chie (孔令傑), male

The children all have the generation name Ling (令) in their names to indicate that they are 76th generation descendants of Confucius.

One of Kung's sons went by the English name of David and was fluent in English. He was born in 1917.

Source (edited): "http://en.wikipedia.org/wiki/H._H._Kung"

Jiang Jianqing

Jiang Jianqing (Chinese: 姜建清; pinyin: *Jiāng Jiànqīng*; born February 1953) is the current Chairman of the Industrial and Commercial Bank of China Limited (ICBC).

Biography
Jiang graduated from Shanghai University of Finance and Economics in 1984, and later obtained his master's and doctor's degrees from Shanghai Jiao Tong University. In 1993, Jiang was appointed as the vice president of ICBC Shanghai Branch. In 1995, he became the president of Shanghai Municipal Cooperation Bank. He started serving as the president of ICBC Shanghai Branch in 1997, and in July 1999, he was promoted to the vice president and vice Party chief of ICBC. From February 2000 to October 2005, Jiang served as the president and CPC Party chief of ICBC. In 2005, when ICBC began to reform towards a public listed company, Jiang became the Chairman of Board of Directors, also the CPC Party chief..

Jiang has served as governor of the Shanghai Bank and the Pudong Subsidiary Bank. His research interests include theoretical and practical bank innovation, and corporation theory of both industrial and financial capital. He is the author of numerous articles including "Technical Revolution in American Banking Industry".

He was an alternate member of the 16 CPC Central Committee and is currently an alternate member of the 17th CPC Central Committee.

Source (edited): "http://en.wikipedia.org/wiki/Jiang_Jianqing"

Jing Shuping

Jing Shuping (simplified Chinese: 经叔平, July 1918 – September 14, 2009) was a Chinese businessman who founded the Minsheng Bank, the first privately owned bank to open in the Communist People's Republic of China, in 1996.

Jing Shuping graduated from the former Saint John's University in Shanghai in 1939. He was Chairman of the All-China Federation of Industry and Commerce and Vice Chairman of the CPPCC until 2002, and held the rank of a national leader of China. He also became a director within the China International Trust and Investment Corp, which is now known as the CITIC Group, the Chinese government's state-owned investment group.

Jing founded Minsheng Bank in 1996. He resigned as chairman of the bank in 2006 citing declining health. However, he remained the honorary chairman of the bank following his retirement. Additionally, Jing opened China's first law firm, consulting firm and accounting firm since the 1949 Chinese Revolution.

Jing Shuping died on September 14, 2009, in Beijing at the age of 91.

Source (edited): "http://en.wikipedia.org/wiki/Jing_Shuping"

K. P. Chen

K. P. Chen (Chinese: 陳光甫, pinyin: *Chen Guangfu*) (b. 1880—d. July 1976) was a Shanghai-based Chinese banker and State Councillor, was a great innovator, as one of China's most successful entrepreneurs in the twentieth century, and was particularly influential in the financial and business world of Shanghai.

In fact, in "Banking in Modern China: Entrepreneurs, Professional Managers, and the Development of Chinese...", the author, Linsun Cheng says, "It is almost impossible to describe any significant innovation in the history of modern Chinese banks without mentioning K.P. Chen's name." This unassuming looking gent was the founder of the first modern Chinese savings bank, a travel agency, as well as the China Assurance Corporation Ltd. On Monday, Mar. 18, 1940, Time Magazine described him thus:

"Middle-aged Banker Chen (University of Pennsylvania '09) looks so much like a Westerner's idea of a Chinese banker that wily and subtle-minded Americans have difficulty in believing he is as simple and direct as he is. Of average height, moderately fat, bespectacled, careful, shy of the press, close-mouthed (in the Calvin Coolidge rather than Sumner Welles sense), he has no hobbies, makes no picturesque Oriental remarks, works 24 hours a day at the unglamorous business of cementing U.S.-Chinese trade relations, and considers Chinese repayment of U. S. loans his personal responsibility. His pride: that China has repaid $2,300,000 of her previous $25,000,000 loan, is now, because of U. S. needs for tung oil and tin, ahead of schedule."

The most important elements in his success were his American education and connections; his sense of professionalism (demonstrated by his opposition to official interference); his ability to compete and collaborate with foreign firms; his desire to innovate and explore various business strategies; his skill at obtaining community and professional support; and the unity of Chinese bankers.

Early life

K. P. Chen was born in Dantu, Jiangsu province in China in 1880. He was born into a family with little education. He caught the attention of compradores of a foreign firm who decided to sponsor his education in America. He graduated in 1909 with a BSc. degree from the Wharton School at the University of Pennsylvania in Philadelphia.

After graduation, as part of the sponsorship agreement, he worked as an intern in an American bank for a year. He then returned to China where he joined the Nanyang Quanyehui (the Nanjing South Seas Exhibition, imperial China's first attempt to join the great European powers in hosting an international exposition, which showcased to the world both China's modernization and her cultural heritage).

Career

The Jiangsu Bank
K. P. Chen began his China banking career in 1913, when he joined a provincial government bank, the Kiangsu Provincial Bank, as its General Manager. There, he introduced something new nearly every day, believing innovation necessary for success.

He broke with tradition and moved the bank's headquarters from Jiangsu to the banking capital of Shanghai, made loans on credit of goods rather than personal credit and invited Western accountants to regularly audit the bank's balance books.

The bank established warehouses for its commodities lending operations, the first to do so in China.

He did all this in just a year, after which he was forced to resign when he refused to disclose the names of the bank's customers to a local warlord.

The Shanghai Commercial & Savings Bank (The Shanghai Bank)
With 80,000 Yuan in initial capital, K. P. Chen, together with some others including President of the Chinese Red Cross, Zhuang Dezhi, founded The Shanghai Commercial and Savings Bank, in Shanghai in June 1915, and was appointed its General Manager. Comparatively, their initial capital was so small the bank became known as "the Little Shanghai Bank".

His guiding principle was "service to society, support for industry, and prosperity to enhance international trade" and he made sure that his staff must be very polite and patient with their clients, small depositors. In his address to his staff in Qingdao branch, he emphasized that they must appreciate their customers business—whether for one or 100 Chinese dollars—must do their best to give their customers convenience, and must be friendly to businessmen. He said "the customer's psychology always favors a busy place," because the sight of a busy firm will make people trust it and claimed that the aim of The Shanghai Bank was to serve society and not just make a profit. So, even though some services would not be profitable, they still had to be offered. Chen Guangfu xiansheng lüezhuan (The short biography of Chen Guangfu, Taipei: Shanghai shangye chuxu yinhang, 1977, p. 31).

Innovation seems to have come naturally to K. P. Chen. It did not stop with the Kiangsu Bank. At The The Shanghai Bank, contrary to what other banks were doing at the time, he concentrated on attracting deposits from the public instead of notes issuance.

K. P. Chen was the first to introduce "one dollar" accounts, encouraging savings among individual members of the greater public and took the lead in introducing many different types of savings programs.

The Shanghai Commercial and Savings Bank's motto, very reflective of Chen's values, was "service to society, support for industry, and development of international trade."

In 1928 The Shanghai Bank handled over 6 million Yuan in foreign exchange and became the number one private bank handling foreign exchange in China. The Chartered Bank of India, Australia and China became upset because of The Shanghai Bank's efforts to promote their foreign exchange business, and decided to refuse The Shanghai Bank's foreign exchange contracts. In retaliation K. P. Chen refused to accept contracts from the Chartered Bank and made this known to the Shanghai banking community through The Shanghai Bankers Association and The Shanghai Foreign Bankers Association, whom he rallied to his cause. Eventually the Chartered Bank came to cooperate with the Shanghai Bank through the mediation of a third party.

In 1931 he created a special trust department in the bank initially to rent out safety deposit boxes but later on including insurance and real estate operations among other things.

He traveled all over China. In the 1930s K. P. Chen would go into the Chinese countryside and attempt to make small farmers "banking-conscious", as observed by a Chartered Bank manager who accompanied Chen on one of his stints. "Don't go to Sinkiang. It's a very hard trip—even dangerous. And when you come back, no one will believe what you find there." he once told a Time Inc.'s Nank-

Travel Service Department of the Shanghai Commercial and Savings Bank

In 1923 K. P. Chen was treated badly when booking his passage at a British-run travel agency. On returning to Shanghai he decided to establish a travel service department within his bank to compete with the foreign travel agencies.

Having made the necessary preparations he submitted a proposal to the Ministry of Communications under the Northern Warlords Government (1912–1927), asking for permission to establish a travel service department and to sell train tickets on a commission basis.

Whilst the proposal was vociferously opposed by the many foreigners occupying important positions in many Chinese railways build with foreign loans at the National Railway Through Transport Conference, it was finally adopted thanks to the support of General Director of Communications Ye Gongche and others, and on August 1, 1923, the Travel Service Department of the Shanghai Commercial, the first of its kind run by Chinese compatriots, was born in the Banks Building on Ningpo road. It operated on a trial basis and opened only to those from "polite society" instead of to the wider populace, providing a comparatively limited business scope.

Its official opening ceremony was held on June 1, 1927 and the Shanghai Commercial and Savings Bank travel department was formally registered as the China Travel Service. Unfortunately, the average daily turnover in the next few months was too low to cover costs. This embarrassing situation provoked a series of complaints from the board of directors and Chen was obliged to make a thorough reshuffle.

With a total investment of US$50,000, the travel agency was separated from its parent company and had to take on the whole responsibility for its profit and loss from then on. Chen Xiangtao, once an official from the Shanghai Public Communications Bureau was assigned the post of general manager. In April 1928, it changed its name to China Travel Service (holdings) Co. Ltd. (abbreviated as CTS (holding)). The year 1931 was the heyday for the CTS, they won the right to deal in European train tickets for Chinese traveling overseas. In the same year CTS opened up more than 20 chain hostels around the country and its annual profits reached more than US$4 million.

The CTS halted its travel service during the War of Resistance against Japan (1937–45) but was unable to recover after the Communist takeover in 1949. Along with the management of the Shanghai Commercial and Savings Bank, the CTS evacuated to Taiwan, but was unable to resume operations. It declared bankruptcy in Taipei in July 1954 and retreated from the arena, but its epoch-making contribution to the Chinese Tourism Industry is still dwelt upon with great relish.

The mainland assets of the CTS were seized by Communist authorities, and today its successor is one of the state-owned large-scale lead enterprises managed by the State-owned Assets Supervision and Administration Commission of the State Council. The core business of CTS (holdings) includes travel, industry invests (steel and iron), the related real estate development and distribution trade.

The Three Musketeers

K. P. Chen cultivated close relationships with Li Ming (founder and CEO of Chekiang Industrial Bank and Chairman of the Shanghai Bankers Association), and Chang Kia-ngau who like he was, represented a new generation of modern bankers.

Half of his initial capital for the The Shanghai Commercial and Savings Bank came from Li's sources.

In 1916, both K. P. Chen and Li Ming stood up for Chang Kia-ngau and accused the government of wrongfully issuing the order when Chang's Bank of China's Shanghai office got into trouble for refusing to obey the governments order to suspend banknote remittance. After this incident, the Bank of China was able to assert its independence from the Yuan Shih-k'ai regime in Peking and started nearly two decades of tremendous growth as China's largest private bank.

K. P. Chen initially became close to Chang Kia-ngau when he became a private financial consultant to the Bank of China at the time between leaving the Kiangsu Provincial Bank and the founding of The Shanghai Commercial and Savings Bank.

Probably because of his tiny initial capital, K. P. Chen received a long term interbank deposit of 50,000 Yuan from Chang's Bank of China as reserve capital encouraging close cooperation between the two banks. Chen and Chang shared a vision of using private capital to develop and modernize the country.

Liu Hongsheng, Insurance and The China Development Bank

In 1927 K. P. Chen teamed up with Liu Hongsheng (1888–1956) to establish an insurance company. Three years later Liu Hongsheng mortgaged his new eight-story group office building to K. P. Chen to raise the capital for launching The China Development Bank.

China's Wartime Finance Advisor

K. P. Chen was head of China's Currency Stabilization Board.

During World War II, the Shanghai Commercial and Savings Bank was devoted to consolidating the economy. In order to solve the financial problems, K. P. Chen represented the government of the Republic of China and negotiated with U.S.A. for loans. Some agreements were made:
- 1936: US-China Gold-Silver Agreement
- 1938: $25,000,000 Export-Import Bank loan
- 1939: Tung Oil Loan Agreement
- 1940: Tien Tin Loan Agreement

In 1938 when the Chinese Ambassador Wellington Koo called on U. S. Secretary of the Treasury Henry Morgenthau to seek financial aid, the U. S. Secretary told him it might be advisable for the Chinese Government to send K. P. Chen (whom Morgenthau had negotiated with in the past) to America to enquire after credit for the purchase of flour and grain goods.

In 1939 Finance Minister H.H. Kung, through K. P. Chen, endeavored to obtain assistance from the American Commercial Credit for the purchase of four airplanes, badly needed by the China National Aviation Corporation. K. P. Chen also participated in concluding a contract at Detroit to purchase 1,000 trucks from General Motors and Chrysler for the Chinese government.

Reputation was important to him and he always made sure he kept his promises and by so doing, demonstrated integrity and ensured that China met its commitments.

Time Magazine on Monday, Apr. 6, 1942 reported that "Shy, determined Chinese financier K.P. Chen stuck a feather in his cap last week. From Chungking he wired Manhattan's Universal Trading Corp. to pay the final installment on a $22,000,000 Export-Import Bank loan smack on the tung-oil barrel head—nearly two years before the last installment on the loan was due." This showed U.S. Treasury officials that China could do business even when Japan controlled its coast. When he sought to borrow money from Washington in 1938, democracy was not considered good security but tung oil, essential in high-grade paints and varnishes, was. To make this work he founded Universal Trading Corp. in Manhattan to manage tung-oil sales, budgeting one-half of the proceeds to repay the debt. He also organized Foo Shing Trading Corp. in China to gather and ship the oil.

K. P. Chen made outstanding contributions in stabilizing the monetary system and raising funds for war of resistance.

After the Communist takeover of mainland China, K.P. Chen followed the Kuomintang-led government to Taiwan, though his Shanghai Commercial and Savings Bank was unable to reestablish its headquarters until 1954. In 1964, the bank was allowed to resume operations. It was the only private bank from the mainland which was allowed to resume commercial operations after the retreat to Taiwan. In 1976, K.P. Chen was succeeded by Chu Ju-tang as chairman of the bank.

Close Shave

In December 1941, K. P. Chen together with Finance Minister and Vice Premier H.H. Kung, his wife Soong Ch'ing-ling and her sister, Madame Sun Yat-sen were caught in Hong Kong when war erupted in Asia. Amid a torrential downpour of bombs and artillery shells, K. P. Chen, Kung, and Madame Sun, were hustled into a plane, flown over the Japanese lines and set safely down, 200 miles inland. (From the Dec. 22, 1941 issue of TIME magazine).

Public Office

On April 17, 1947 Generalissimo Chiang Kai-shek, President of the National Government of the Republic of China nominated K. P. Chen to membership of the then new state council.

Champion of Human Capital Development

K. P. Chen believed in the power of people and saw his investment in their development as an investment in the future profits of the bank.

He approved an annual budget of 12,000 tael in silver and invited a former manager of the Deutsche-Asiatische Bank to lecture his staff on the theory and practice of foreign exchange.

He set up an educational fund to send senior managers to America to continue their education and practice advanced banking skills there.

The bank had a global business network through its overseas representative offices managed by its senior managers.

Other positions

- K. P. Chen, whose bank had been involved with the cotton industry since its early days, served as Chairman of the Cotton Control Commission or CCC. He was close to T.V. Soong, the Minister of Finance and Founder and Director of the National Economic Council, whose idea it was to make private entrepreneurs and capital a vital part of the CCC's nation-building efforts, and had long been involved in state-private projects sponsored by Soong.
- K. P. Chen was the dynamic chairman of the Universal Trading Corporation (UTC), a wholly owned subsidiary of China's Nationalist Government, formed for the purpose of promoting Sino-American foreign trade. Chen, a successful, self-made capitalist entrepreneur, believed that UTC could be the perfect vehicle for his stewardship of China's postwar economic reconstruction. He also placed a premium on Sino-American cooperation and communication.
- K. P. Chen was Chairman of the China Committee of International Chamber of Commerce. He was also Chairman of China's Foreign Trade Commission.
- K. P. Chen was a signatory to the 1938 appeal for U. S. support by 10 Chinese Associations in Shanghai following the occupation of Manchuria by Japan. (United States Department of State / Foreign relations of the United States diplomatic papers, 1932. The Far East Volume III (1932) -- The Far Eastern crisis: occupation of Manchuria by Japan and statement of policy by the United States, pp. 1–754)
- K. P. Chen was a major financier of industrial projects. Often working together with others, he set up various textile, metals and trading companies. He was a member of the board of Fan Xudong's Yongli Group of Companies.

Source (edited): "http://en.wikipedia.org/wiki/K._P._Chen"

Li Ruogu

Li Ruogu (born January 1951) is Chairman and President of the Export-Import Bank of China (China Eximbank).

Biography

Li Ruogu graduated with a Masters in Law from Beijing University in 1981 and a Masters in Public Administration from Princeton University in 1983. He was briefly an assistant professor at Beijing University before joining the People's Bank of China in 1985. In the 1990s, Li spent a year as an International Monetary Fund economist and four years at the Asian Development Bank as the chief representative of China, as well as acting as liaison to the African Development Bank. He was at the position of Deputy Governor in charge of international affairs in the People's Bank of China before moving to the current position in late 2005.

Source (edited): "http://en.wikipedia.org/wiki/Li_Ruogu"

Li Zhaohuan

Li Zhaohuan (Chinese: 黎照寰; 1898-1969), was a Chinese educator, politician and banker. He is well-known as former President of Chiao Tung University (aka Jiaotong University; 交通大学) and the last President of Hangchow University.

Biography

Li was born in Hainan County, Guangdong Province in 1898. Li's style name was *Yaosheng* (曜生).

Li studied in the United States. He obtained BA in economics from Columbia University, and MA in politics from the University of Pennsylvania.

Li became a member of Tongmenghui. Li was the general manager of the Hong Kong Industrial Bank (香港工商银行) and Chinese Merchants Bank (华商银行). Li was the director of the Guangzhou-Kowloon Railway Administration Bureau. Li was a professor of several notable universities, including Chiao Tung University (current mainly Shanghai Jiao Tong University in Shanghai, Xi'an Jiaotong University in Xi'an, and National Chiao Tung University in Hsinchu, Taiwan), Saint John's University, the University of Shanghai (different from current Shanghai University). Li was pointed the Vice-president of Chiao Tung University in June 1929. In October 1930, Li became the President of Chiao Tung University. Li served for Chiao Tung University for 12 years.

Li was a counselor for the Minister of Finance of the Republic of China, and the Vice-minister of the Ministry of Railway of ROC. Oct 1927, Li was pointed the Vice-gonernor of the National Central Bank of ROC.

After 1949, Li was a professor and the last President of Hangchow University (a root of current Zhejiang University in Hangzhou).

Li was a Vice-chairman of the first to fourth Shanghai People's Political Consultative Conference.

On 16 September 1968, Li died in Shanghai.

Source (edited): "http://en.wikipedia.org/wiki/Li_Zhaohuan"

Lim Peng Siang

Lim Peng Siang (林秉祥) or **Lin Bengxian** (1872–1944) together with his brother Lim Peng Mao of Lin Bingmao, through their Ho Hong Group of companies,, founded in 1904, had interests in banking, shipping, parboiled rice, oil mills, cement, coconut and other businesses. President of Singapore Chinese Chamber of Commerce from 1913 to 1916 except for 1914 when he was Vice-President. He had close ties with the Hong Kong Fujian Chamber of Commerce and he and his brother Lim Peng Mao (Lin Bingmao) were listed as honourable chairpersons of that association between 1930 and 1941. Member of the Chinese Advisory Board between 1921 and 1941. His Ho Hong group built circa 1910 was the most diversified group in Malaya at the time. Peng Siang Quay in Singapore is named after him.

Origins

Lim Peng Siang, the son of Lim Ho Puah and the only daughter of Wee Bin, the founder of Wee Bin & Co. He was born in Amoy, Fujian, China in 1872. After receiving his education in Chinese, he travelled to Singapore when he was still very young. Like his father, Mr. Lim Peng Siang was a naturalised British subject and had been so since 1902. He received private tuition in acquired most of his English education from private tuition. He was a student at the St. Joseph's Institution.

He joined the firm of Wee Bin & Co., which was then under the management of his father, Lim Ho Puah, and eventually rose to its head before setting out to start the Ho Hong Group. He took over the greater part of the firm's business, including the large steamers when the firm of Wee Bin & Co. was liquidated in 1911

Shipping

In 1914 Lim Peng Siang founds the Ho Hong Steamship Company Ltd. In 1936 Lim Peng Siang sells most of his shares in Ho Hong Steamship to OCBC.

Banking

He founded the Chinese Commercial Bank in 1912 together with other members of the Singapore Hokkien business community. Together with Lim Boon Keng, Seow Poh Leng and others he founded the Ho Hong Bank in 1917. In 1932, The Chinese Commercial Bank and the Ho Hong Bank merged with the Oversea-Chinese Bank to form the Oversea-Chinese Banking Corporation, later known as OCBC.

Ho Hong Group

By the 1910s the Ho Hong group was

the most diversified group in Malaya. Among the other Ho Hong concerns which owe their existence to Mr. Lim Peng Siang are The Ho Hong Steamship Co. Ltd., The Ho Hong Oil Mills Ltd., The Ho Hong Parboiled Rice Mill, The Ho Hong Bank Ltd., and the Ho Hong Portland Cement Works Ltd. He had other schemes and the necessary machinery ready for a bucket-making factory and for the reclamation and development of several big pieces of swampy land in a big industrial area in the immediate neighbourhood of Singapore Town.

Leadership of Trade and Mercantile Organisations and Public Councils

He was ah honourable chairperson of the Hong Kong Fujian Chamber of Commerce between 1930 and 1941. He was one of the leading men among the Chinese merchants of Singapore and was greatly respected by the community. He took an active interest in the formation of the Singapore Chinese Chamber of Commerce and has been one of its Presidents. He was a member of the Chinese Advisory Board, on which he has served for many years as one of the representatives of the Hokien (Fukien) community, and was a J.P. He was a director of a number of public companies, including the Central Engine Works Ltd. and the Central Motors Ltd. In his later years he was of a retiring disposition in so far as public activities were concerned, and though offered a seat on the Legislative Council on several occasions he had been obliged to decline it, having to give his whole attention to the numerous industries which he had built up.

A Clinic In Amoy

"About six months ago, a Mr Lim Peng Siang, an intimate friend of mine, doing banking and shipping business in Singapore, Hongkong, Amoy and Shanghai, returned to his village for a rest. One day a neighbour paid him a visit. This man had leprosy but thought it to be some kind of skin disease. Mr Lim then sent him to me for treatment. The response to treatment was very quick, he was so pleased that even now, he is used as an attraction for the sufferers of the same disease to come for treatment. With my cooperation a clinic was established by Mr Lim in his native place, Shima, two hours by launch from Amoy. Today there are about 85 receiving treatment."

Benefactor

It will be seen therefore how great a benefactor Mr. Lim Peng Siang has been to Singapore. It is hardly necessary to mention here how much a country depends on industry and shipping for its wealth and importance. It can be clearly seen to what extent Mr. Lim Peng Siang has contributed to both these factors. From time to time severe competition with other steamship lines reduced deck-passage rates to a ridiculously low figure and it also meant heavy loss to the firm: but this proved a boon to thousands of the labouring classes who were enabled to leave their homes in China and come to the Straits Settlements and the Netherlands East Indies to supply the labour market.

During the Great War he proved his patriotism by working hard in helping to raise money for the various funds, besides himself liberally contributing to such funds. He was never known to refuse help to a deserving cause, and innumerable were the charities to which he liberally contributed. He set an example worthy of being followed by the rising members of the Chinese community.

Source (edited): "http://en.wikipedia.org/wiki/Lim_Peng_Siang"

Xiang Junbo

This is a Chinese name; the family name is Xiang.

Xiang Junbo is the current chairman of Agricultural Bank of China Limited and has been since January 2009. He has also obtained a PHD in law from Peking University, which is situated at Haidian District in the western suburb of Beijing.

Source (edited): "http://en.wikipedia.org/wiki/Xiang_Junbo"

Xiao Gang

Xiao Gang (Chinese: 肖钢; pinyin: *Xiào Gāng*; born 1958 in Ji'an, Jiangxi) is currently chairman of the board of directors of Bank of China Limited and Bank of China (Hong Kong) Limited. From 1998 to his appointment to his current (as of 2005) position in 2003, he was a deputy governor of the People's Bank of China, the central bank of the People's Republic of China.

Biography

Xiao Gang has been Chairman of the Board in Bank of China Limited since August 2004. He used to serve as Head of Bank in the Company. He is also Chairman of the Board in BOC Hong Kong (Holdings) Ltd. Xiao also served as Assistant Head and Deputy Head of the People's Bank of China (PBOC), Head of PBOC-Guangdong Branch, General Manager in China Foreign Exchange Center. He graduated with a Master's degree in International Economic Law from Renmin University of China in 1996.

Source (edited): "http://en.wikipedia.org/wiki/Xiao_Gang"

Zhang Youyi

Zhang Youyi (1900 – 1989) (also spelled Chang Yu-I), was the first wife of the Chinese poet Xu Zhimo. Zhang was famous in her own right as a banker and educator.

Biography

Marriage and children

- Hsu Chi-kai (1918 –)
- Hsu "Peter" Bide (1922 – 1925)

Source (edited): "http://en.wikipedia.org/wiki/Zhang_Youyi"

Zhuang Xiaotian

Zhuang Xiaotian (Traditional Chinese: 莊曉天, Simplified Chinese: 庄晓天), is a Chinese politician and senior banker. He is the first President of the Shanghai Pudong Development Bank.

Biography

Zhuang was born in 1933 in Zhenhai County (current Beilun District), Ningbo, Zhejiang Province. 1945, he graduated from Weidou Elementary School. He went to Shanghai with his brother. He is a graduate of Shanghai University of Finance and Economics.

Zhuang is the former vice mayor of Shanghai. He was mainly in charge of Shanghai's commerce, trade and industry. He's the current President of the Foundation for Shanghai Elderly, the President of the Shanghai Urban Development Foundation, the Chief Supervisor for the Shanghai Charity Foundation, the President of Shanghai-Ningbo Economic Association (上海宁波经贸促进会), and the President of the Shanghai-Ningbo Chamber of Commerce (上海宁波商会).

Source (edited): "http://en.wikipedia.org/wiki/Zhuang_Xiaotian"